Praise for *The Passion Paradox: When You Feel Miles Apart and Still Love Each Other*

The Passion Paradox is **a wonderful guide for couples to find the sweet spot between passion and joyful comfort.** We get to explore the corners of our psyches that we often hide from our partners due to confusion, vulnerability, or fear of losing them. **Dr. Chalmer shares stories that we can relate to**, and exercises that help us open up these potential sore points gently so that we can look at them in kindness and **find the intimacy that we are truly looking for.** — **Katrina Bos**, author of *Tantric Intimacy: Discover the Magic of True Connection*

Dr. Chalmer's book *The Passion Paradox* offers **a way forward for people who are stuck in painful relationship limbo**. Whether you're reeling from an affair, struggling with intimacy issues, or have simply grown apart, Dr. Chalmer guides you to take stock, learn the skills you need, and move forward, whether that means staying together or splitting up. **I recommend this book for individuals, couples, and the people who are helping them heal.** —**Janis Abrahms Spring, Ph.D.**, bestselling author of *After the Affair*

Dr. Chalmer's book *The Passion Paradox* provides an **immensely helpful** approach to re-viewing one's relationship. His workbook's ideas and exercises rest on the **essential dignity of each person** in a relationship, and his compassion, wit, and embracing of human imperfection underwrite this **exceptionally useful, practical, growth-supporting** workbook. **What a wonderful contribution to our field!** —Jean Pieniadz, Ph.D., Clinical Psychologist/Psychoanalyst, and Co-author, *Dialogue Therapy for Couples and Real Dialogue for Opposing Sides: Methods Based on Psychoanalysis and Mindfulness*

Praise for *Betrayal and Forgiveness: How to Navigate the Turmoil and Learn to Trust Again*

A guiding light for the betrayed, Dr. Bruce Chalmer's wise and compassionate book escorts you on a courageous journey toward understanding and forgiving others and yourself, after even the most devastating upheavals. –**MB Caschetta**, author of *A Cheerleader's Guide to Spiritual Enlightenment*

Whether you're a client or a clinician, Dr. Bruce Chalmer's latest book *Betrayal and Forgiveness* offers **spectacular insight** into the rich landscape of couples therapy. **I highly recommend Betrayal and Forgiveness for clinicians and clients alike.** –**Jane Kast, M.A.**, psychologist

Bravo! *Betrayal and Forgiveness* **is a clear, easy to read, and relatable book for anyone struggling with these topics.** It gives clear guidance to those who have been stung by betrayal, those who have betrayed, and the therapists and coaches who work with them. I highly recommend this book to anyone seeking to understand how to navigate the aftermath of betrayal and for those who yearn to heal.—**Karin Calde, Ph.D., CPC**, Relationship and Self-Development Coach and host of podcast, "Love is Us"

"Forgiveness is an inside job" is a powerful and necessary concept Dr. Chalmer motivates the reader to embrace. –**Dr. Deborah S. Miller**, author of *More Than Sorry: 5 Steps to Deepen Your Apology After You Have Committed Infidelity*

Praise for *It's Not About Communication! Why Everything You Know About Couples Therapy is Wrong*

Dr. Bruce Chalmer's book *It's Not About Communication* takes the reader "behind the curtain" of the whole couples therapy process. He demystifies the often mysterious and unknown experience of therapy so that couples know what to expect as soon as they walk through the door. Compassionate and informative, along with using a bit of humor, Dr. Chalmer shares his wealth of knowledge that comes from years of treating couples. **I recommend this book to both therapists and couples alike** who are looking for a roadmap of the couples therapy process. –**Dr. Alyson Nerenberg**, author of *No Perfect Love- Shattering the Illusion of Flawless Relationships*

If you're stuck in your relationship this book may be the catalyst you need to have the relationship you want. — Susan Bratton, "Intimacy Expert to Millions"

Unlike so much of the help on offer these days, Dr. Chalmer offers an engagingly and endearingly clear path to this way to feel at home in the universe. **A breakthrough book for couples ready at long last to brave reality in all of its paradoxical splendor.** –**Jeremy Sherman**, author of *What's Up With A**holes? A Beginner's Guide to Advanced Psychoproctology*

Written in an **accessible, conversational style**, this book provides the unexpected solution to relationship problems in couples. Based on three key ideas and illustrated with case examples from clinical practice, Dr. Chalmer highlights the steps to lasting change. **A worthy resource for both couples and therapists who want to be effective.** –**Dr. Paul Foxman**, author of *Dancing With Fear*

Praise for *Reigniting the Spark: Why Stable Couples Lose Intimacy, and How to Get It Back*

Reading this book is like breathing fresh Vermont air—refreshing, inspiring, down-to-earth, and filled with grounded wisdom that emerges from decades of practice as a therapist with hundreds of couples… I am especially inspired by his willingness to bring spiritual lives—religious and nonreligious—into the conversation, exploring with couples what matters most to each of them, while dealing with life's inevitable uncertainties and struggles. –**Peggy Sax,** psychologist and Executive Director of Reauthoring Teaching

This book is concise, but it is **so well written that it feels like we are sitting in his office or laying on his couch, talking about what we want and asking how we can get there.** He shows us how to lay a foundation for intimacy and trust that will connect us to our partner for years to come. He also makes us take a look at all the reasons we should and shouldn't get married. And if you're already embroiled with a cheater? Well, he shows us how to navigate that situation too, and decide whether or not a fractured relationship is worth salvaging or whether we should simply walk away. – **janandheather.com**

I was hooked on this book from the very first sample I read of it. I appreciated that Dr. Chalmer doesn't shy away from difficult topics like sex, trauma, and anxiety in relationships and that he acknowledges the difficulties those situations present in maintaining relationships. I've even recommended this book to someone for precisely that reason. **I give *Reigniting the Spark* five stars.** – **carijehlik.com**

The Passion Paradox

When You Feel Miles Apart and Still
Love Each Other: A Workbook

Dr. Bruce Chalmer

Also by Dr. Bruce Chalmer

Understanding Statistics (1986)

Reigniting the Spark: Why Stable Relationships Lose Intimacy, and How to Get It Back (2020)

It's Not About Communication! Why Everything You Know About Couples Therapy is Wrong (2022)

Betrayal and Forgiveness: How to Navigate the Turmoil and Learn to Trust Again (2024)

The Passion Paradox:
When You Feel Miles Apart and Still Love Each Other: A Workbook

Copyright © 2025 by Dr. Bruce Chalmer

No part of this publication may be reproduced, distributed or transmitted in any form or by any means, including photocopying, recording, or other electronic or mechanical methods, or by any information storage and retrieval system without the prior written permission of the author, except in the case of very brief quotations embodied in critical reviews and certain other noncommercial uses permitted by copyright law.

Published by Someware Publishing

Cover design by Annemarie Lamprecht

ISBN Paperback: 979-8-9907504-3-2

Table of Contents

Introduction 1

Chapter 1: How's Your Relationship? 9

Chapter 2: Stability and Intimacy: The Two Golden Gifts 19

Chapter 3: What Happened to the Spark? 33

Chapter 4: Reconsider Your Relationship 43

Chapter 5: Should You Call It Quits? 53

Chapter 6: How Do You Turn It Around? 67

Chapter 7: What is Faith? 83

Chapter 8: Should You Try Couples Therapy? 97

Chapter 9: Will Your Partner Try Couples Therapy with You? 103

Chapter 10: Being the Change: Introduction 115

Chapter 11: Parenting 121

Chapter 12: Stepparenting 129

Chapter 13: Marriage 133

Chapter 14: Finances 141

Chapter 15: Sex 147

Chapter 16: Betrayal 155

Chapter 17: Addiction 161

Chapter 18: Relationships with In-Laws 169

Chapter 19: Religion and Politics 175

Chapter 20: Everything Else 181

Chapter 21: How to Split Up 183

Acknowledgements 191

About the Author 193

Introduction

Where Did the Passion Go?

What happened to the passion you used to have in your relationship? And how can you get it back? You still love each other—at least, you think so. But where did the feeling of being "in love" go?

Remember when you couldn't keep your hands off each other? When sexual energy buzzed between you? When you glowed with pleasure and desire when you came into each other's presence? What happened to all that?

If your problem is that your partner is abusing you, or humiliating you, or controlling you, you don't need this book—you need a safety plan. Get out of the relationship.

What I'm talking about in this book is relationships that aren't abusive but have somehow gone cold. Maybe you do well together in the business aspects of life—running the household, taking care of the kids, paying the bills—but you miss that sense of connection you once felt. Maybe you're squabbling about trivia, or constantly irritated with each other, or walking on eggshells. Or maybe you've just given up trying to talk about anything important.

And what about your sex life? What was once exciting and new has become routine, or maybe non-existent. You don't seem to be able to talk about it, much less improve it. It's just too scary to go there.

And it's painful—maybe painful enough that you're wondering if the relationship can survive. A lot of the couples in this situation who come to work with me in couples therapy are on the verge of divorce or separation. The prospect of staying in a relationship without intimacy, sexually or otherwise, is awful.

Well, here's the good news and the bad news.

The good news is your problem is normal. I don't mean it's just what you have to expect, so suck it up, though that's what some couples do. I just mean it's normal, in the sense that it happens as a developmental stage in many long-term relationships. Couples lose the sense of passionate connection due to very normal processes—you'll be learning about them in this book. Doesn't sound like good news, does it? But the good part is that once you recognize what's happening, you can change it. You're not stuck with it forever. That's the good news.

And even better, you've come to the right place. This book will guide you through the changes you need to make.

The bad news is that making those changes is scary. It's scary, precisely because you've lost the connection as a consequence of avoiding anxiety—so the solution will involve tolerating that anxiety. It's scary because you'll have to face your own fears: fear of your own desires, fear of challenges to your core beliefs and values, and fear of the loss of the relationship.

In other words, **you'll need courage to do this work.**

What I'm Assuming About You

I realize there's a vast array of reasons why you might be drawn to this book. Your situation is unique in some ways, because you're unique in some ways. So I'm not assuming much about who you are, what your particular situation is, or why you're reading this. You'll see examples of couples having lots of different issues, and you'll relate to some of them more than others.

But I am assuming some very basic facts about you:

- **You're essentially sane.**

- **You're intelligent.**
- **You're essentially good at heart.**

When I say you're essentially sane, I don't mean to make light of serious mental health issues. I just mean that if you were having some sort of psychotic break or manic episode, you probably wouldn't pick up this book.

The same reasoning applies to the assumption that you're intelligent. I don't mean merely that you're not cognitively impaired; of course you wouldn't be reading this if you weren't capable of understanding it. I mean you're intelligent in the sense that you're not insistently closing your mind to possibilities you hadn't considered. If you've read this far, you're willing to consider that you can learn something you didn't know. That's what I mean by intelligent.

And you're essentially good, not evil. Yes, you've sometimes done things that you realize were morally wrong, or hurtful to others. But you care about it. You aspire to be a basically good person. Again, if that's not you—if you're actually a sociopath—you wouldn't be reading this.

I'm pretty sure you were already making those assumptions about yourself. But **I invite you to extend those same assumptions to your partner.**

Yes, I know you might have trouble assuming those things about your partner. Maybe they *aren't* sane or intelligent or good. But I urge you to start with the assumption that they are all of those as you do this work, for two reasons.

First, if you think your partner is crazy or unintelligent or evil, you're probably wrong. You probably think those things when you're pissed off, and judgements you make when you're pissed off are notoriously unreliable. You sometimes act unreasonably, and so does your partner, especially when you're upset with each other. I'm not saying your anger is unjustified—I'm just saying you can't rely on assessments you do when you're in a rage.

Second, even if it turns out that your partner is having serious mental health issues, or turns out to be insistently closed-minded, or is a sociopath, you'll have much more room to consider your options if you don't assume those things from the start. As I mentioned earlier, if you're in danger, get out. But if you're not in acute danger, give yourself some time and space to learn what you need to learn. And that means being open to the possibility that what you and your partner are going through isn't as simple as just one of you being the problem.

You may notice that my example couples are all hetero and monogamous. That doesn't mean I'm assuming you're in a monogamous hetero relationship. I think a lot of the ideas in this book are applicable to all sorts of relationships, and I've been told as much by gay and lesbian couples I've worked with. But my experience is overwhelmingly with monogamous hetero couples, and I don't want to pretend otherwise. I'm leery of claims of general applicability. If you're in a different kind of relationship, apply the ideas that work, and ignore the ones that don't. Of course, I can say the same to anyone using this book.

How to Use This Book

This is a workbook. So prepare to work.

The book has three parts. In the chapters of Part I, you'll take stock of your relationship. You'll use the Stability and Intimacy Assessment to examine your relationship, and you'll learn about why stability and intimacy matter. You'll see why many loving relationships lose their spark, how some couples are able to keep the spark alive for decades, and learn about how that can happen. You'll reassess your relationship, and get a clear sense of what's working and what isn't. And finally, you'll face the question of whether to call it quits or keep working on it.

In the chapters of Part II, you'll work on the skills you need to fix your relationship. You'll learn the key skill that makes all the others possible, and what you need to practice to develop the mindset to move forward. You'll consider whether couples therapy could be helpful, and if necessary, how to invite your reluctant partner to go to couples therapy with you.

In the chapters of Part III, you'll work on "being the change." This means applying the skills you've learned to handle the most common challenges couples face: issues in your sex life, infidelity, financial problems, parenting differences, religious and political differences, and more.

When you see a **bold print instruction** like this:

Write down your impressions…

it means you're being asked to do a particular task—usually, answering some questions or writing some thoughts about yourself and your relationship.

You'll need a way to write your answers and impressions. I recommend the old-fashioned way using pen and paper, if you can. You can also dictate or type using a device, but you learn more by going slowly, so take your time even if you're typing or speaking.

The prompts are numbered. As you respond to each prompt, note the page and prompt number so you can refer back to the prompt when you're reviewing what you wrote.

Don't worry about crafting your answers—just write what occurs to you. You're not writing for publication.

The ideas in this book will help you—but you need to engage with those ideas for yourself. **The more you put in, the more you'll benefit.** This might be scary at times. Be prepared to challenge your beliefs, accept some uncertainty, and open your mind to possibilities you haven't considered.

By Yourself or Together with Your Partner?

You can use this book by yourself. But it's even better if both you and your partner work on it. It's best to get a copy for each of you (yes, I know that's self-serving of me, but it does work better that way). Most of the questions you'll be considering are intended for you to work on by yourself, at least initially, so the two of you will be working independently much of the time. It's a lot easier if you don't have to pass the book back and forth. Of course, if you have the eBook or audiobook version you can have it on two devices.

If you're working on it by yourself, at various times you'll also be asked to consider inviting your partner to participate in considering some questions. If you're not ready to do that, this book will help you figure out why, and open up possibilities for working on your relationship issues together. Whether or not you feel able to talk to your partner about this work, you'll still benefit from it. And your own learning and growth will benefit your relationship too.

Ready? Let's get to work.

Part I

Take Stock

Chapter 1

How's Your Relationship?

The Stability and Intimacy Assessment

On the following pages is a series of questions designed to help you think about your couple relationship.

Do the questions in order, and work on them by yourself, not with your partner. If an item doesn't apply to you, just leave it blank.

As you answer the questions, feel free to write down any thoughts or questions that occur to you.

You'll probably want to download and print the form—one copy for yourself, and maybe one for your partner. Scan the QR code on this page, which takes you to brucechalmer.com/sia.

Ready? Go.

Part A: Stability Think about your relationship, and for each item rate how much you agree with the statement. If an item doesn't apply, just leave it blank.	How much do you agree? 0 = not at all, 10 = completely
1. I feel I can count on my partner to be there when I need them.	
2. I think my partner feels they can count on me to be there when they need me.	
3. I feel committed to the relationship.	
4. I think my partner feels committed to the relationship.	
5. We seem to agree about being monogamous.	
6. We seem to agree about how neat things should be.	
7. We seem to agree about where we want to live.	
8. We seem to agree about how to parent our kids, or whether to have kids.	
9. We seem to agree about how to handle finances.	
10. We seem to agree about how to handle religious observances.	
11. We seem to agree about how to handle extended family relationships.	
12. I feel confident that our relationship will last.	
13. I think my partner feels confident that our relationship will last.	
14. Overall, I think my relationship is stable.	

Part B: Intimacy Think about your relationship, and for each item rate how much you agree with the statement. If an item doesn't apply, just leave it blank.	How much do you agree? *0 = not at all,* *10 = completely*
1. I feel that I can bring up concerns with my partner if something is bothering me.	
2. I think my partner feels they can bring up concerns with me if something is bothering them.	
3. I feel loved by my partner.	
4. I think my partner feels loved by me.	
5. I feel desired by my partner.	
6. I think my partner feels desired by me.	
7. I feel we can talk about what we like and don't like in our sex life.	
8. I feel satisfied with our sex life.	
9. I think my partner feels satisfied with our sex life.	
10. I feel I can tell my partner about my dreams or fantasies.	
11. I think my partner feels they can tell me about their dreams or fantasies.	
12. I feel that my partner handles it well if I disappoint them.	
13. I feel that I handle it well if my partner disappoints me.	
14. Overall, I feel satisfied with the level of intimacy in my relationship.	

Part C: Meta-Assessment Think about your relationship. How much do you agree with the statement?	How much do you agree? 0 = not at all, 10 = completely
1. I am comfortable asking my partner to do this assessment, and to compare our answers and talk about them together.	

Gather Your Thoughts

The sections of this workbook like this one labeled "Gather Your Thoughts" are where you'll do the work that will help you cope with your situation, make sound decisions, and generally feel better. **So don't rush through these sections!**

You'll notice that there's no scoring system for your responses to the Stability and Intimacy Assessment. There's no classification scheme that tells you which supposed archetypes your relationship is enacting, or which personality types you are or aren't compatible with, or which love languages you're conversant in, or which attachment style you're stuck with.

That's because this assessment is designed to get you to open your mind, not close it.

Now that you've done the assessment, think about the questions below. **Write down what comes to mind.** Don't worry about getting them "right"—just write your impressions as they occur to you. I'll be giving you my take on some of these topics later, but it's important that you think about them first from your own perspective, as they apply to your own relationship.

1. How do you understand the difference between stability and intimacy in general? Why are they both important? Or are they? (I think they are, but that doesn't mean you have to!)
2. You rated how you feel about the overall stability of your relationship in the last question of Section A. Thinking about your answer now, what were the biggest factors that led you to your overall rating?
3. You rated how you feel about the overall level of intimacy in your relationship in the last question of Section B. Thinking about your answer now, what were the biggest factors that led you to your overall rating?
4. What sort of skills do you think people need for stability in a relationship? How effective are you in using those skills? How effective is your partner?
5. What sort of skills do you think people need for intimacy in a relationship? How effective are you in using those skills? How effective is your partner?
6. Some of the questions in the assessment might have caused you some anxiety. Which questions seemed the scariest, if any? What was scary about them? Don't try to resolve your worries now—just take note of them.

Are You Okay Asking Your Partner to Do the Assessment?

Now consider your answer to the question in Section C, where you rated how comfortable you are about asking your partner to do the assessment and compare your answers.

This is where this chapter becomes a sort of "choose your own adventure" book. Follow the directions in *italics*.

Thinking about it now, are you willing to ask your partner to do the assessment?

If no—if you're not willing to ask your partner to do the assessment—skip to the section below headed "No!"

If yes, keep reading.

Yes!

Okay, you rated yourself as willing to ask your partner to do the assessment. **Go for it! Ask your partner to do the assessment.**

If your partner agrees to do the assessment, give them a fresh copy and ask them to do the assessment independently, as you did. Then get together to go over your answers. Once you've done that, move on to the next section headed "How Did It Go?"

If your partner declines to do the assessment, or won't discuss their answers with you, skip down to the section headed "Still No!"

How Did It Go?

Great—you've invited your partner to do the assessment, and they did it. And you've gone over your answers with each other.

How did it go? **Write down your thoughts about the questions below.** You could do this separately or together, but the questions are for each of you to consider—you don't have to agree on your answers. Take your time on these!

1. What did you learn about your partner that surprised you? Were there items where their answer was worrisome to you? Were there items where their answer was a pleasant surprise? Pay particular attention to the items that ask about what you think your partner feels about something: Part A items 2, 4, 13; Part B items 2, 4, 6, 9, 11. How accurate were your guesses?
2. What did you learn about your partner's impressions about you? Pay particular attention to the items that ask about what your

partner thinks you feel about something (same items as above). How accurate were their guesses?

3. Did comparing your answers change any of them? If your own guesses about your partner were off, would you change your guesses now that you've talked to them? (Oddly enough, you might not in some cases—maybe you think your partner isn't being completely candid about their own response.)

4. Similarly, if your partner's guesses about how you feel differed from your own answers, is it possible they're more accurate than you thought? Is it possible they've noted something about how you feel that you weren't fully aware of yourself?

5. Think about item 1 in Part B, which asked you how much you agree with the statement, "I feel I can bring up concerns with my partner if something is bothering me." Item 2 in that same part asked you to guess how your partner feels about bringing up concerns with you. Now that you've both done the assessment and talked about your answers, would you change how you responded to those two items? After all, your conversation might have involved sharing concerns. Do you now feel more confident that you can share concerns with each other and have the conversation go okay? Or less confident? Or about the same?

6. Now reassess your answer to the item in Part C, where you rated how comfortable you are asking your partner to do the assessment and compare your answers. Of course, you've now done just that. Overall, how comfortable would you be asking your partner to do something similar in the future? That's another way of asking, how did this exercise go overall?

Skip to the next Chapter. (Or keep reading this chapter if you're curious about how you might have handled it if your partner hadn't agreed to participate.)

No!

You're here because you weren't willing to invite your partner to do the assessment and talk about it with you. **Now consider:** Would you be willing to tolerate the discomfort and risk asking them anyway?

If yes, go back up to the section headed "Yes!"

If no, read on.

Still No!

Okay, if you're following the "choose your own adventure" instructions in this chapter, you're here at this section for one of two reasons. Either (a) you're not going to invite your partner to do the assessment, or (b) you did invite them, but they declined to do it or talk to you about it.

If it's (a), think about why you're not asking your partner. If it's (b), think about why your partner might have declined, and try to imagine what they might say if they were asked to explain why they declined.

Write down your impressions as you think about what's making either you or your partner reluctant to get together on this. You might want to start by writing, "I'm worried about approaching my partner to do the assessment because..." or "I think my partner is reluctant to participate because..." Here are some possibilities to consider:

1. Are you concerned that even bringing up the idea with your partner would lead to an argument or deep freeze? Are you worried that they might be shocked that you're bringing up something that could suggest that you're having doubts about the relationship? Can you imagine them saying, "I thought we were fine. Why are you bringing this up?" Or are you worried they might get angry, counterattack, or shut down?

2. Are you concerned that if you did share your answers with your partner, that would lead to an argument or deep freeze? Do you worry that your partner will reject what you're saying, or get defensive?
3. Maybe you're thinking they might not like the idea of doing an exercise you're suggesting just because you're suggesting it.. Are you worried they'll take your suggestion as implicit criticism? That you're somehow trying to maneuver them into therapy? (We'll talk in Chapter 9 about how to invite a reluctant partner to try couples therapy with you.)
4. Do you think your partner might be worried about your reaction if they say no? Does your partner have reason to worry about your reaction if they frustrate you? Are you worried about your own ability to manage frustration? If your partner did say no to doing the assessment, how did you handle it? Were you generally gracious, curious, open to understanding their concerns? Or were you angry, punishing, shut down? Or some combination?
5. Are you concerned that if your partner did the assessment and shared their answers with you, their answers might upset you? Are you worried about what you might discover if you ask?
6. If you did suggest that your partner do the assessment and they said no, could you talk with them about why you're suggesting it? This would involve your being honest about your concerns about the relationship. Could you let go of the idea of inviting your partner to do the assessment and just tell them about your concerns?

Still No?

How are you feeling now that you've thought about it some more? Of course, if going over your concerns has helped you be comfortable enough to risk asking your partner to do the assessment, even if they might have declined once, go for it.

But if you still find the prospect of bringing up your concerns with your partner to be too risky, you're clearly having intimacy problems in your relationship (which I imagine you already knew).

If that's where you're at, let me share bad news, good news, and uncertain news.

The bad news is that if you can't somehow fix those intimacy issues, you're headed for trouble—or more trouble—in your relationship. We'll talk in Chapters 2 and 3 about the symptoms of intimacy problems.

The good news is that you don't have to be stuck. This book is all about finding ways to turn things around so you can risk opening a channel to intimacy.

The uncertain news is that there's no way to know for sure how it will turn out. You might discover, or re-discover, a fulfilling, passionate relationship with your partner—and I hope you will. But you might end up deciding to separate, or to accept a less than fulfilling relationship and stay together for the sake of stability. There's just no way to know for sure which way it will go.

If you can handle that uncertainty, read on. You'll learn valuable lessons that will serve you well going forward, in your present relationship or in some future one.

Chapter 2

Stability and Intimacy: The Two Golden Gifts

Why Do Stability and Intimacy Matter?

Now that you've done the assessment, and possibly compared your answers with your partner's, let's go deeper. Why are stability and intimacy so important in a relationship? The more you understand these ideas, and the more you can apply them to your own relationship, the better your ability to turn things around.

In this chapter you'll meet some couples I've worked with (of course, names and identifying details have been changed to maintain confidentiality). First, let's talk about what I mean by stability and intimacy, and why they are such key concepts.

Why Do People Get Into Couple Relationships?

Why couple up at all?

Yes, we're mammals, and mammals reproduce sexually—at least, that's still mostly true as I write this!. But lots of mammals, and other species that reproduce sexually, do just fine reproducing without forming a pair-bond between the male and female. For those species, the male is just a sperm donor. There's no such thing as a couple as humans understand it.

Besides which, lots of people form couple relationships with no intention of having children. What about people past child-bearing age? What about gay couples? What about people who specifically don't want to have children? Why do they couple up?

It's not just about reproduction. You already knew that—because whether or not you have children, you're not doing this workbook just because you want to stay coupled to have kids.

Then why *do* we form couples? What needs are we trying to fulfill?

Two Golden Gifts

You've already been introduced in Chapter 1 to the central idea of this book: The two needs we're trying to fulfill by forming a couple are **stability** and **intimacy**.

I've referred to stability and intimacy in some of my previous books as "the two golden gifts," because when they are sufficiently fulfilled in your relationship, your relationship will be precious to you.

And you'll both want to stay in it.

I'm using the term "needs" carefully here. I don't mean that stability and intimacy are simply desires, though they are indeed desirable. I mean they are needs, in the sense that if they aren't sufficiently fulfilled, the relationship doesn't function and eventually dies. **You need both stability and intimacy for your relationship to survive just like you need food and water for your body to survive.**

Let's see why that's true.

Stability

Meet Devon and Kara.

When I met them, Devon and Kara were both 30 years old. They'd been together—or more accurately, they'd been trying to be together—for about a year. When they came to my office for their first appointment, they had just found out a couple of weeks previously that Kara was pregnant. She was clear that she intended to have the baby, and that the father was Devon. He acknowledged that he was the father.

How would they know if the therapy was helping? (That's my usual opening question.) They'd be able to stay together for more than a couple of months without one or the other leaving, refusing to speak for days on end, or cheating. That had been their pattern since the first time they had moved in together.

The way the pattern often played out was some variation on this theme: They'd have some kind of disagreement, often when one or both had been drinking. This would devolve into a nasty argument, which in turn would expand to encompass all the other nasty arguments they had had previously and had never resolved. One or the other of them would storm out, sometimes staying elsewhere for a week or two, during which they might get involved sexually with someone else. They would both regret separating and get back together. Rinse and repeat.

You can see why Kara and Devon are my poster couple for stability issues.

I'm using the term "stability" in its usual sense. When things are stable, they aren't shaky. Stable relationships feel solid. Essentially, when your relationship feels stable, you're not worried about it. The longer you go without worrying about it, the more confidence you develop in that basic stability. When you have that confidence, the occasional bit of shakiness, say, a minor disagreement, doesn't amount to anything significant.

Conversely, when the relationship keeps breaking down, you're worried about it even when it seems to be going well. Any momentary challenge turns into a full-fledged crisis—which in turn causes you to worry even more going forward. It's a nasty cycle.

You can compare Kara and Devon's cycle to what happens when someone has a panic attack. The diabolical thing about a panic attack is that once someone has had one, whatever originally set off their fear reaction is largely irrelevant. The panic attack itself is so terrifying that it becomes its own stimulus! I've often noted that if panic attacks had been invented by a person, we'd call that person an evil genius. Hijacking your necessary survival functions to cause suffering—that's worthy of a James Bond arch-villain.

Fortunately, if you've had panic attacks you can learn to spot the cycle and head it off, so that it loses its power over you. But when it's a couple that's caught in the cycle, rather than an individual, it's often harder to head it off, because each of their panic reactions exacerbates the other's.

You might imagine how Devon and Kara might have answered the questions on Part A of the Stability and Intimacy Assessment. Counting on your partner to be there when you need them? Feeling committed to the relationship? Confident that the relationship will last? Their responses would have shown lots of agreement: agreement about how unstable their relationship was.

The Essential Skills You Need for Stability

What skills do you need for your relationship to be stable?

Essentially, you need to act in ways that avoid or minimize anxiety. In other words, you need to not freak out your partner. Or yourself, for that matter.

In practice, this means that you need to adhere to the expectations you have of each other. So you don't cheat, or behave in ways that cause your partner to worry that you might cheat. You show up when you say you will, and do what you say you're going to do. You speak to your partner with respect, and don't speak ill of them to others.

Of course, you expect similar consideration from your partner. But you also recognize that you're not perfect and neither are they. So you handle their occasional lapses with grace, and you hope your partner will grant you that same grace. You apologize when you blow it, even as you extend to yourself the grace you want from your partner.

The skills of stability are a lot about character and maturity. You act with integrity, which means you assume responsibility for the choices you make and are willing to hear and examine ways you might have caused hurt. And when you are able to recognize your own fallibility, you can extend compassion to your partner when they are fallible too.

Stability, Sanity, PTSD, and Sobriety

Remember what I said I'm assuming about you, the reader, in the Introduction? I said I'm confident that you're essentially sane, intelligent, and good, and so is your partner.

That first one, that you're essentially sane, is particularly critical for stability. As I mentioned in the Introduction, I'm assuming you're not in the midst of some sort of psychosis or mania, the kind of thing that so distorts a person's sense of reality that they're apt to perceive threats and react to them even when there aren't any. This, of course, is hugely destabilizing to a relationship.

But there are two other far more common conditions that also result in distorted perceptions of reality.

One is Post Traumatic Stress Disorder (PTSD). As I'm sure you know if you or a loved one are affected by PTSD, panicking or dissociating when you're reminded of past trauma can cause big problems in a relationship. PTSD isn't a malfunction; it's your brain trying to protect you. But untreated PTSD can wreak havoc on stability in relationships.

The other common destabilizing condition is inebriation. If you're drunk, or stoned, or otherwise chemically besotted, your reactions are apt to be destabilizing also.

I routinely ask couples in their first session if they have any concerns about substance use, either their own or their partner's. Sometimes, of course, they'll report that indeed, one or both has a history of use that has caused serious problems. Sometimes one or both attends a group such as AA or another 12-step program.

Of course, substance use isn't crazy. People use alcohol or pot or whatever because it works. And sometimes a couple can use substances together in a way that enhances their experience.

But even when they both say that their use is not problematic, they'll often add that their worst moments with each other seem to happen when one or both have been drinking. I'm not trying to imply that substance use is inherently destabilizing, but I am inviting you to consider the possibility.

This is a good time to examine your own relationship to both of those conditions.

If you have untreated PTSD, have you worked on it in therapy? Have you avoided working on it, in hopes that you can just tough it out?

If you're having stability issues similar to Kara and Devon, are those issues partly related to your substance use? Have you avoided thinking about that possibility? If so, why?

If you do recognize that you have PTSD, or a substance use problem—or both, since they often co-occur—**you need to act on it.** (Or, of course, you can continue to ignore the problems, read on, and then wonder why this book isn't working for you. I don't recommend that approach.)

What does acting on it look like? That's up to you. For PTSD, it means finding a therapist with competence in that area, and doing the work. If your substance use is at the point where abstaining would require detox, you should get medical help. If you've tried to change your use pattern before and haven't succeeded, you should find a counselor and/or support group to help you. You probably knew that already.

You're Probably Pretty Good at Stability

All of that said, **I'm guessing you're pretty good at the skills you need for stability**.

Wait a minute. As I've often commented to couples I work with, nobody makes a first appointment to see me just to tell me how stable their relationship is. And the same reasoning applies to you. If you didn't have any worries about the stability of your relationship, you wouldn't be using this workbook.

Then why do I think you probably have pretty good stability skills?

The answer is a corollary to those three assumptions I'm making about you: you're essentially sane, intelligent, and good. If you're all of those, you're blessed with those sources of stability. And the fact that you're working through this book, and you've made it this far, implies that you're willing to look at possibilities you haven't considered and take responsibility for your own part in your situation.

Those are signs of maturity and character. Those are essential stability skills.

Another reason I think you're pretty good at stability skills: As the subtitle of this book indicates, this is a workbook for people who love their partner, but feel miles apart. Just the fact that you can recognize that you still love your partner, even though things have become painful, is a sign that you've formed a relationship that has lasted this far. And that requires stability skills.

Of course, I could be wrong—maybe your problems are mostly about lacking stability skills. But read on anyway, because even as you're working on improving your stability skills, you'll also need to develop your capacity for the other golden gift. You'll need to develop the skills of intimacy.

Intimacy

Time to meet another couple.

When I started working with them, Madison and Ian were in their late forties. They'd been married for 18 years, and had two teenage children. The event that brought them to my office was a conversation they had a month before: Madison told Ian that she loves him, but isn't "in love" with him anymore, and she suggested that they open the relationship to the possibility of ethical non-monogamy. For Madison, this meant that they'd stay married, but each would be free to have sexual relationships with other people. They would set ground rules so that there wouldn't be any deception, and each of them could specify how much they did or didn't want to hear about the other's extramarital connections.

Ian's first reactions to this were a mix of shock, anger, and grief. He had sensed some distance between them for a while, especially evident in their nearly nonexistent sex life, but had no idea that Madison was no longer "in love" with him. He was still in love with Madison. Hence his shock reaction.

And to find out that Madison wanted to open the relationship, allowing for sex with other people? Essentially, that she wanted to cheat, but not call it cheating? He was disgusted by the idea. This wasn't what he signed up for. Hence his anger.

The grief set in soon after, as he realized that his objections would get him nowhere with Madison. If he couldn't agree to what she wanted, he might lose her altogether. In some ways, he recognized, he had already lost her.

It was Madison who suggested that they try couples therapy, as their conversations seemed to go round in circles. Their web search led them to my website right around the time I had posted a link inviting people to test out the Stability and Intimacy Assessment. When they contacted me to make an appointment, they had already done the assessment and compared their answers.

As you have probably guessed, their responses in Part A, the questions about stability, reflected general agreement about how they want to live, parent their children, handle finances—basically, they were aligned on those issues. It was Part B, the questions about intimacy, that clarified for them how they ended up in the crisis they were in.

What is Intimacy?

People use the term "intimacy" in a lot of ways. Sometimes, it's just a synonym for sex. I'm using the word in a broader sense. Here's my definition:

Intimacy for a couple is when you're each present and honest with yourself and each other.

To be present with yourself means to be physically tuned in to your body and senses, emotionally aware of how you're feeling, cognitively alert and responsive, and spiritually grounded. That last part, spiritually grounded, means to be clear about your own essential validity—that sense that whoever you are, however fallible, you're not a mistake. (Another word for that sense of validity is faith, which we'll talk about later on.)

That's a tall order. No one can be present in all of those ways all of the time. And then to be able to be honest with your partner, and to be open to your partner's honesty, is an even taller order.

Which means that no couple can be intimate 24/7.

The Essential Skill You Need for Intimacy

Earlier I pointed out that the essential skills for stability are all about keeping the anxiety levels—yours and your partner's—low. For stability, you need to act in ways that don't freak out yourself or your partner. That means doing what you can to avoid raising anxiety.

But the essential skill for intimacy is tolerating anxiety, rather than avoiding it.

That's the central thesis of this book, so I'll repeat it in bold.

The essential skill for intimacy is tolerating anxiety, rather than avoiding it.

When I point that out to couples, they often look at me quizzically. Isn't intimacy supposed to feel good? What does that have to do with anxiety?

Well, of course intimacy feels good, often. Moments of deep connection, great sex, delighted sharing of lovely experiences—those are all examples of intimacy, and they feel wonderful.

But intimacy isn't only about sharing sweet moments. What about if you want to complain to your partner about something they're doing or not doing? And what if you've complained before, and the conversation hasn't gone well? What about if those conversations ended up in frustrating fights or days-long deep freezes, never resolving the issues? The more you've had difficulty bringing up a complaint, the more anxious you'll be about bringing up another complaint.

Moderate Annoyance and the Emotional Bank Account

Here's another way of stating the basic skill needed for intimacy: **You need the ability to be moderately annoyed.** Annoyance is basically a form of anxiety. If you can tolerate moderate annoyance without crossing over into panic, you'll be willing to be honest about how you feel, and you'll be able to hear your partner's honesty without freaking out.

When things are going generally well, an annoyance is just an annoyance. When things aren't going well, annoyances feed the cycle of panic. Since annoyances are inevitable—let's face it, you and your partner and I and everyone else are all annoying sometimes—the ability to be moderately annoyed is an indication that you're not on the edge of freak-out. And the more you can handle annoyances without freaking out, the less you'll be afraid of addressing them both honestly and compassionately.

One of my favorite metaphors about tolerating anxiety is the "emotional bank account."

You know what happens when an actual checking account gets overdrawn, right? It's not only that you have pissed off the person you paid with a rubber check. It's even worse, because the bank hits you with an overdraft fee, and you're even more in the hole than you were before.

The emotional bank account works similarly. Whenever you and your partner have a pleasant interaction, you've made a deposit. When you have a nice, healthy balance, you can afford the occasional withdrawal—a minor argument or moment of disconnection stays minor, and you still have plenty of positive left in the account.

In fact, when you have a healthy balance in the emotional bank account and you do encounter one of those moments of disconnection—say, your partner speaks sharply to you—you're inclined to wonder what's happening and respond with concern rather than anger. "Ouch—that was intense. Is something bothering you? Can I help?" Or even, "Ouch—I'm really sorry, I guess I had that coming. What can I do better?" Whereupon your partner apologizes for speaking so sharply, and you can actually talk about what was bothering them in a spirit of mutual generosity.

But when you've had a run of withdrawals, and the balance is depleted, even a minor annoyance results in a big fee. Now you're in the hole, and there's no reserve. It's scary to be in the hole, which means both you and your partner are even more prone to overreact to each other. "Don't talk to me that way! There you go again, you're always yelling at me." And you proceed to argue about how you're arguing, rather than talk about whatever bothered one of you in the first place. The overdraft fee keeps making more overdraft fees. It's a nasty cycle.

Gather Your Thoughts

Write down your impressions as you consider these questions:

1. Do you recognize the overdraft cycle in your own relationship? Do you have disagreements that devolve into arguments about how you're speaking to each other? If so, how did each of you play your role in the cycle? Pay particular attention to your own role. For example, did you object to how your partner spoke to you without acknowledging their original complaint? This isn't about whether you or your partner were justified in your behavior; just notice how the cycle works to perpetuate itself.
2. Think about an occasion when one of you raised some sort of objection, and the two of you were able to resolve it amicably. (If you can't think of such an occasion, go back further in time. There must have been one if you've been together long enough to be reading a book like this.) As you think about it now, what made it possible for the two of you to hear each other and come to agreement? Did it feel like a compromise, a capitulation, a win-

win, or something else? If you can recall, how did you feel afterward about your partner and the relationship?

Intimacy Isn't Only About Annoyances

It's not only raising complaints or handling annoyances that can spike your anxiety. What about sharing your dreams, fantasies, uncertainties, anything that you worry might surprise or repel or just mystify your partner? **What if your sharing raises doubts in your partner about who you are?** What if they react badly? What if they think your sexual fantasy is repulsive? What if they think your idea about moving somewhere is a sign of a faltering relationship? What if they think your dream of starting a business is just unrealistic nonsense?

If you're going to be honest with your partner, you'll need to risk raising anxiety, both theirs and your own. If you don't want to risk raising anxiety, you'll learn to keep your thoughts, dreams, and fantasies to yourself.

And keeping your innermost desires hidden means avoiding intimacy.

You can try that for a while—in fact, I'm guessing you're reading this because you and your partner have been doing just that. And as you've probably figured out, that strategy ultimately fails.

Understanding just why and how that strategy fails is the beginning of healing. In the next chapter we'll look at how that happens.

Gather Your Thoughts

Now that we've talked about stability and intimacy in more depth, could you explain them in your own words? **If you can, find a friend or relative—someone other than your partner—and tell them**

about what you've been working on. Explain the idea of stability and intimacy as needs that require different skills.

By explaining the ideas to someone else, you'll be improving your own understanding. And, of course, you'll learn from the other person's responses.

I guessed above that you're reading this because you and your partner have been unintentionally avoiding intimacy in the interest of protecting stability. As you think more about stability and intimacy in your own relationship, how accurate is my guess?

Write down your impressions.

Chapter 3

What Happened to the Spark?

The Death Spiral for Intimacy

Let's revisit Ian and Madison.

Like so many of the couples I work with—maybe like you and your partner—Ian and Madison had been practicing the skills of stability for years. They were basically compatible with respect to things like how and where they want to live and parent their children, which means they didn't have to argue much about those issues. They weren't confronting obvious deal-breakers. There was no infidelity, and neither one had concerns about their own or their partner's substance use.

As their relationship progressed, and they began to build a life together, stability became even more important. Having kids put the need for stability at the forefront of their relationship. Both Madison and Ian steered clear of anything that might rock the boat too much.

Of course, no matter how compatible a couple may be, they are still two different people. Disagreements will arise, sometimes important enough that they can't just ignore them or agree to disagree.

Madison and Ian had various disagreements in the early years of their relationship. But when Madison thought about when things started to get difficult, one particular event seemed to be at the source of the developing rift between them.

It was the day after the birth of their second child, and Madison and the baby had just come home from the hospital. Madison's mother was scheduled to arrive the next day to help take care of their two-year-old. As Madison remembered it in our session, an hour after they got home from the hospital Ian asked her if it was okay if he went that afternoon to play golf. She "went ballistic" (her description), and Ian apologized and stayed home.

Ian remembered it differently; he said he just wondered if it might be okay to go out for a couple of hours while the two-year-old was napping. But he agreed that he shouldn't have even asked that, and that's why he apologized.

That event alone didn't wreck their connection. But for Madison, it was the first time she remembered doubting whether Ian had her back. And any time he seemed unaware of her needs, she was reminded of those doubts. Whenever he would ask about doing something for himself, she would feel conflicted. She didn't want to be "that wife" who would deny her husband leave to have fun, but she couldn't shake the sense that he didn't really have her interests at heart.

Ian started to dread checking with her about what he might want to do. It seemed to him like he was irredeemably guilty of being inconsiderate, no matter how much he did for her and how much he tried to show her he cared. So he stopped checking in with Madison, and just made plans on his own, telling her about them only when necessary. This just confirmed Madison's fears.

When a couple starts to dread talking honestly, they've shut down intimacy. That's how the death spiral operates.

And for Ian and Madison, as for many couples, this lack of intimacy was reflected in their sex life.

Intimacy and Sex

I mentioned when I was defining intimacy that the term as I'm using it is much broader than simply referring to sex. In fact, there are lots of ways to be intimate that aren't sexual at all. Close friends and family members can be deeply intimate, in the sense of being present and honest with each other.

But for a partnered couple for whom sex is part of their relationship, how their sex life is going is often a pretty good indicator of how their intimate connection is going more broadly. Not always, but often. And even when a couple's sex life has been impeded by factors unrelated to their relationship—say, medical issues—how they handle those issues often reflects how they handle other forms of intimacy as well.

We'll be talking about sex more specifically in Chapter 15. For now, Madison and Ian's story can be helpful in understanding how intimacy issues can result from a self-reinforcing cycle.

Maybe you'll notice something familiar in their story.

A couple of months after their second child's birth, when Madison had healed up enough to be cleared for sexual activity, Ian wanted to get their sex life back on track. Both of them reported that their sex life had been good before that second child came along.

But now something had changed for Madison. She was annoyed by Ian's attempts to interest her sexually. It seemed to her that he expected any affectionate gesture to turn into sex. She tensed up at his approach. And she started to avoid even small acts of physical contact with him, because she felt like it would just lead him on when she had no interest in sex.

Ian got more and more frustrated with Madison's rejection. No matter what he did for her, she saw it as just an attempt to get inside her pants. She was right that he wanted sex with her—not as a transaction, but as an expression of intimacy. After numerous rejections, he stopped trying to be intimate in any way. This strengthened Madison's impression that Ian didn't really want to be with her at all unless it was for sex, which made her even less interested in any sort of intimate connection.

When we talked about this in our couples sessions, Madison recognized the irony. She had always considered Ian's attraction to her to be a strength of their relationship. She didn't want to be irritated by it. But she didn't know how to feel differently.

Ian just felt caught in a trap. Madison resented his desire for her, but even if he could pretend that he didn't desire her, that would just be confirmation of her fears.

Gather Your Thoughts

How much of Madison and Ian's story sounds familiar to you?

Not every couple can identify an iconic turning point the way Madison did (for her, it was the events on the day she came home from the hospital after giving birth to their second child). But many can. **Write down your impressions as you consider these questions about your relationship:**

1. When you think back over your intimate connection—sexual or otherwise—when was it strongest? What do you remember about that time that reflected a strong intimate connection?
2. If your connection seems weaker now, what's missing from when it was strong?

3. Do you recall any particular incidents that seem to have weakened the connection?
4. How does your sex life with your partner correlate with your intimate connection more generally?
5. How do you think your partner would respond to these questions? Feel free to talk to your partner about them.
6. If you did talk to your partner about these questions, what did you learn?

Symptoms of Lack of Intimacy

I mentioned in Chapter 2 that **stability and intimacy are both needs, not merely desires**. If either one is inadequately satisfied, the system breaks down.

Inadequate stability threatens the relationship by definition: to say that a relationship is unstable means precisely that it's threatened. Recall Devon and Kara, whose relationship was continually teetering on the brink of breakup.

What about lack of intimacy? What happens to a couple when intimacy is shut down?

Consider a plant that grows from a seed. Say the seed fell from a nearby oak tree onto fertile soil. It germinates and sprouts and starts to grow. When it's just a seedling, someone comes along and paves a sidewalk over it. For stability, of course—it's a lot easier to walk on a sidewalk than on bare ground.

That seedling won't just sit there. It will try to crack the sidewalk, or die trying. You've probably seen plants growing through cracked pavement.

For the seedling, roots provide stability, so it won't blow over in the breeze and lose connection with its source of nutrients. But intimacy is the energy for growth. Living organisms are driven to be intimate with their environments, to grow and adapt. Failure to grow is to die.

That's true for any living organism—indeed, that's one way of defining what makes something alive. Like the seedling, each of us strives to be intimate with our environment. And when intimacy is blocked, we try to crack through whatever pavement is in the way. Or die trying.

What does cracking the pavement look like in a couple where intimacy has been blocked?

Sometimes, as for Ian and Madison, it's a nonexistent sex life. Sometimes one or both partners has an affair. Sometimes one or both partners become deeply depressed. Sometimes a couple finds themselves arguing about anything and everything except the genuine differences that they're too afraid to talk about. Sometimes the couple goes through long deep freezes, punctuated by nasty fights. Sometimes one partner blindsides the other by suddenly abandoning the relationship.

Eventually, lack of intimacy itself becomes destabilizing.

How Do Some Couples Keep the Spark Alive?

So far the story sounds pretty dismal, doesn't it? As I noted in the Introduction, the processes that lead to the death spiral for intimacy aren't rare or pathological; they're normal! And you're probably reading this because you're caught in some version of that death spiral.

Does that mean that it's inevitable? Are all couples doomed to lose intimacy?

Fortunately, the answer is no. For some couples, the spark stays alive for decades. You might know some couples like that. When you're around them, you can sense the electric charge between them.

I'm not telling you that to make you feel bad that they have something you don't. I'm telling you that because if you understand how they do it, you might discover you can do it too.

How do they do it?

Let's meet Mimi and Jason. They're both in their late 60s, and have been married for 25 years. It's a second marriage for each of them. Mimi had been divorced for five years when she met Jason, who had been divorced for a little over a year.

I don't know Mimi and Jason through my work; they're personal friends of mine. As I've done for clients I've written about, I've disguised identifying details, but they don't mind my using them as examples.

The chemistry between them is palpable. Mutual friends have commented on it. They seem to enjoy each other's presence, and when either one talks about the other you can hear the respect, love, and admiration coming through. Friends who have known them the whole time they've been together attest that it's been like that continuously.

When I asked Mimi and Jason about their relationship, they agreed with my observation that they seem to have cracked the code for maintaining the spark over the long haul. They had somewhat different explanations for how they had managed that feat, consistent with their differing experiences before they met each other.

Mimi attributed their success largely to "finding the right person." She had learned from her first marriage not to ignore the red flags that, in hindsight, she now realized were present early on. That she was divorced for five years before she met Jason was testimony to her willingness to be selective. She knew what she wanted in a marriage, and wasn't willing to "settle." When she met Jason, she knew he was the right one, and time proved her correct.

Jason agreed with Mimi's emphasis on finding the right person as a key factor. But he also recognized how much they benefited from having been through marriages that didn't work out. They were so grateful to be in a warm, joyous, intimate marriage that disagreements don't bother them much—they just work them out without rancor. In terms of the emotional bank account metaphor I talked about in the last chapter, Jason was saying they've maintained a healthy balance.

They also each talked about how their relationship had fostered growth, and continues to do so. I didn't want to ask them for more detail about their intimate life than they wanted to disclose to a friend, but Mimi and Jason both said their willingness to be vulnerable with each other had allowed them to explore their sexuality in ways they never had before. And they said they were still discovering new aspects of themselves and each other, both sexually and more generally.

Are Jason and Mimi lucky to have found each other? I certainly think so, and they each say so too. But their continuing success isn't just luck.

Mimi and Jason are able to keep their marriage vibrant because they've developed the skill of tolerating anxiety, rather than avoiding it.

When I offered this idea to them, Mimi said that her first thought was to disagree, because being with Jason didn't cause her anxiety. But then she remembered times early in their relationship when she would worry about how Jason might react to something she wanted to ask of him, worries she since realized were residue from her first marriage. Rather than stifling her feelings, as she had in her first marriage, she recognized that it was important to speak up.

As it turned out, Jason's reactions were consistently supportive, even if he disagreed with her, so over time she stopped being anxious about bringing up what was on her mind. But it was her willingness to risk honesty—to tolerate the anxiety—that made that positive cycle possible.

Jason recognized the importance of tolerating anxiety rather than avoiding it as a lesson he learned from going through the loss of his first marriage. He had initially been blindsided by his then wife's turning away from him, and only later came to understand how much he had avoided letting himself know how troubled their relationship had become. Surviving that loss helped him put other problems in perspective, which in turn made it easier for him to be open to whatever issues Mimi wanted to raise. And it also taught him not to avoid his own feelings.

Gather Your Thoughts

Write down your impressions as you consider these questions:

1. Do you know couples like Mimi and Jason, couples who have maintained a vibrant connection over the long haul? If so, how do you think they've done it? What do you know about each of them that might contribute to their success?
2. Do you remember a time when your own relationship was like theirs? If so, imagine yourself as an observer watching the two of you when you were out with other people. What would you be seeing that would lead you to sense that this is a couple with a lively intimate relationship?
3. If you do remember a time when your own relationship was like Jason and Mimi's, how were you able to do it? In particular, do you remember how you handled differences that arose between you? Has that changed in more recent times?
4. How do you think your partner would respond to these questions? Feel free to talk to your partner about them.
5. If you did talk to your partner about these questions, what did you learn?
6. If you didn't talk to your partner about these questions, why not? What did you think might happen if you brought it up? Or if you did bring it up and your partner didn't agree to talk about it, why might they have resisted?

Chapter 4

Reconsider Your Relationship

Revisit the Stability and Intimacy Assessment

Now that we've talked about stability and intimacy in more depth, it's time to reconsider your relationship. **Go back to the Stability and Intimacy Assessment** in Chapter 1, or print it out—a copy for yourself and one for your partner if they're willing to do it. Here's the link and QR code again: brucechalmer.com/sia.

As before, do the assessment by yourself. If you're willing to invite your partner to do the same, go ahead and invite them, and when you've both done the assessment get together and talk about your answers.

When you've finished those tasks, read on.

Gather Your Thoughts

Write down your impressions as you consider these questions:

1. Overall, how did it go to do the assessment again yourself? Did you find you've changed your answers from the first time? If so, were the changes due to differences in how you understood the items, or actual differences you've noticed in your relationship, or some combination of those?
2. If your partner did the assessment again, did you compare your answers? If so, how did it go? Did the experience of comparing your answers offer some new perspectives?
3. Think about your answer to the item in Section C, where you rated how comfortable you are asking your partner to do the assessment and compare your answers. Whether or not you actually did that this time, has your answer to that item changed since the first time you did the assessment? If so, why? If not, why not?

Let's Get Specific

You've now done the Stability and Intimacy Assessment twice, and maybe your partner has also. If you're doing this workbook because you're trying to figure out what to do about your relationship, you've probably got a pretty good idea of where the problem areas are. For many people I've worked with, the distinction between stability and intimacy is a new way of understanding what's happening. The work you've done so far has been about developing that understanding.

Now what?

Before we consider what to do to make things better—whether that's by fixing the relationship, or ending it—we need to get into more detail. The rest of this chapter is about common issues that affect stability, intimacy, or both. Understanding how (or if) these issues affect your relationship will be key to understanding how to proceed.

Write down your impressions as you consider each of the items below. Work on this by yourself.

As you'll see, each item consists of a general heading followed by a bunch of questions. You don't have to explicitly answer each question, but even the questions that aren't specifically relevant to you might get you thinking about aspects you hadn't considered.

Spend some time with each general item, even if it's not a problem in your relationship. If a particular issue is not a problem—good news!—write down why. Is it because you and your partner never disagreed on the issue, or you've successfully resolved whatever differences you had, or some other reason?

If a particular issue is a problem, try to identify what your differences are. **Resist the urge to blame either yourself or your partner—just try to understand your respective stances.** Remember, this isn't about solving the problem (yet)—just understanding it.

This task should take you some time. Give it what it needs! The thought you put into this will help you when you get to Part III of this book.

1. Having/Not Having a Child

If you and your partner don't have children, have you talked about whether or not to have children? If you already have one or more, have you talked about whether to have another? This isn't about *how* to parent children (that's another item)—just about *whether* to parent children.

Even if there's no possibility of having more children in the future, to what extent has this decision been problematic in your relationship in the past?

2. Getting Married or Not

If you're not married, have you and your partner talked about getting married? Do you agree on this? If one of you wants to get married and the other is resisting the idea, why does each of you feel the way you do?

If you are already married, were you both equally on board with the idea beforehand, or did one of you convince the other?

3. Where to Live

If you live together, how do you each feel about where you live? This includes considerations about how close you are to extended family, what geographical region you live in (especially in terms of your preferences about climate and culture), what sort of community you live in (urban/suburban/small town/rural), commuting distances, and anything else that occurs to you about your choice of location.

Does either of you wish you could move somewhere else? How did you end up living where you live?

4. Financial Organization

How do you and your partner organize your finances? Do you have separate accounts, joint accounts, or some combination? Do you consider your assets as separate ("these are mine and those are yours"), or as jointly held ("it's all ours") or some combination?

If you keep separate accounts, how much does each of you know about the other's finances? Do you each know how much money the other brings in through employment? Do you each know how much the other has in savings, investments, or debts?

How did you arrive at the arrangement you have? Did you agree on it? Do you know whether you still agree on it? What happens to your financial assets when one of you dies? Have you talked about that?

5. Income and Careers

Does one of you get paid substantially more than the other? If so, how did that happen? Did you come into the relationship already in your respective careers, or have your careers changed over time? For example, if you had children together, did that change how one or both of you are employed? If one of you stopped or reduced outside employment to become the primary caregiver, how did you decide that? What expectations do you each have about how you'll support your family financially?

If one of you is or was in school for a time while the other maintained employment, has that been a source of resentment or conflict? Or have you generally felt united in a common effort?

6. Financial Decisions

How do you and your partner make decisions about major purchases? Do you have an understanding, tacit or explicit, about when you need to consult each other before spending money, and when it's okay to make your own decision and act on it?

Do you each have some money you can spend without consulting the other? Does either of you dread conversations about money, or feel that your partner is often critical of your decisions?

Do differences in your respective income affect how you make financial decisions? For example, does the partner who makes less money feel disempowered, or the partner who makes more money feel resented? Or do you both feel able to express your preferences? Have you talked about that?

7. Addictions and Problem Behaviors

Are you concerned about your own or your partner's use of alcohol or other drugs? Is your partner concerned? Have you talked about those concerns with each other?

Have you found that arguments are worse when one or both of you has been using alcohol or other drugs? Do you sometimes feel that your partner isn't reliable or emotionally present because of their use? Does your partner sometimes feel that way about you?

Do you have concerns about other problem behaviors, such as compulsive gambling or compulsive shopping? Do you wonder if you or your partner is a "sex addict?" Have you talked about those concerns?

If you don't have any of those concerns, is it because there's no problem, or because you're engaging in denial? Note that this doesn't presuppose that there must be a problem; it's just recognizing that people sometimes ignore the signs when there is a problem.

8. Fidelity/Infidelity

Has either one of you been unfaithful, sexually or emotionally? If you have been unfaithful, does your partner know about it? Is it ongoing? Do you suspect that your partner has been or is being unfaithful, but you haven't talked about it, or they deny it?

If you feel there has been infidelity and you've talked about it, do you both agree that what happened represented infidelity? If your agreement with each other is to be monogamous, have you talked about what that means? For example, is looking at pornography a violation? Is masturbation a violation? Could a friendship cross the line into an emotional affair?

If your partner was the one who cheated, how long ago did you find out about it? When you think about it now, how much panic do you feel? Do you feel able to think about why it happened without getting lost in anger or shame? Have you been able to talk to your partner about it?

If you're the one who cheated, do you feel able to think about why you did what you did without getting lost in anger or shame? Have you been able to talk to your partner about it?

If there has been infidelity, to what extent have you rebuilt trust? Does either of you feel like a perennial suspect, or perennial probation officer?

If there hasn't been infidelity, why not? What about your relationship has protected you from infidelity? Is it a matter of luck, or commitment, or something else?

9. Other Betrayals

Have you felt betrayed by your partner, or have you betrayed your partner, in ways besides infidelity? For example, has either of you spoken harshly or lied about the other to friends or family, or lied about significant financial details, or made a decision that impacts both of you without consultation? Have you talked about it with each other?

If there haven't been betrayals, why not? What about your relationship has protected you?

10. Child-Rearing Approaches

If you have children, how often do you argue about how to handle situations involving them? You've almost certainly noticed that the two of you have some differences in style and approach. How have you navigated those differences? How confident are you that you can work them out?

If you're in a blended family (that is, at least one of you is a stepparent), how's that going? How do you manage differences between parenting and stepparenting? Is this a problem area in your relationship, or a source of strength, or some combination? To what extent do issues with ex-spouses about co-parenting affect your current relationship?

To what extent do you and your partner agree about disciplinary approaches? About diet? About which activities to forbid, allow, or promote? About safety concerns? How do you handle differences about those issues?

11. Extended Family Issues

How do you and your partner handle problems that arise with extended families? Are in-law relationships problematic sometimes? Does one of you feel caught between your own family and your partner?

Is either of you experiencing an estrangement from a family member? If so, how does that affect your relationship? Does it sometimes come between the two of you?

11. Religious Practice

Do the two of you agree on religious practice (or lack thereof)? If your religious backgrounds or affiliations are the same, do you practice your religions similarly? Where there are differences, how do you handle them?

If you have children, how do you decide about religious education and practice? How much do you require, and how much do you leave up to the children to decide? Has this been a source of conflict?

12. Politics and Moral Values

To what extent do you and your partner agree about politics, or about hot-button issues that have become politicized? Are you able to talk about those issues and still feel connected to each other? Have you found that you need to avoid some topics with each other, because they lead to painful arguments that you're not able to resolve?

To what extent do you feel you and your partner's moral values are compatible? Does either of you excuse or trivialize conduct that the other considers reprehensible? Are you able to talk about your differences, or does trying to talk about them lead to fights or freezes?

13. Your Sex Life

You were asked about how satisfied you are with your sex life in the Stability and Intimacy Assessment. Now let's consider your sex life in more detail.

Are you having sex as often as you wish, or less often, or more often? How do you think your partner feels about the frequency you're having sex?

If you're having sex with each other at all, occasionally one of you is in the mood and the other isn't. How do you handle those moments? Do you handle those times gracefully, or do they lead to painful arguments or freezes? Or some of each?

How compatible do you feel your sexual desires are? Do you talk with each other about what you like, what you don't like, what you might want to try, or other aspects of preference? If your partner tells you to stop doing something, or change how you're doing it, do you receive that guidance gracefully or resentfully? If you tell your partner to stop doing something, or change how they're doing it, do you deliver your guidance gently or harshly? How does your partner receive it?

Are you concerned that your sexual orientations might not be compatible—for example, if you're a male-female couple, do you worry that one of you is gay? If your sexual orientations are compatible, do you worry that your erotic orientations might not be compatible—for example, if one of you wants to incorporate a particular fetish or kink that the other finds revolting or unacceptable?

Would you call your sex life a strength in your relationship, a weakness, or some of each? If your sex life is a strength of your relationship, why? What have you noticed about how your sex life affects your intimate connection more generally?

14. Intimacy More Generally

How alive do you feel in your relationship? When you encounter your partner, do you feel you can be who you are, or are you walking on eggshells? How alive do you think your partner feels?

How often do you laugh together? How often do you feel that your partner is glad to see you? How often do you feel glad to see your partner?

Are there particular activities that you and your partner enjoy together? If you've been together a long time, have those activities changed? Do you enjoy discovering new things together?

15. Other Issues

If there are issues that come to mind that you haven't yet considered in this exercise (there probably are), think about them now. Describe how they affect your relationship.

Now consider: Are you willing to ask your partner to go through the same items and compare your answers?

If so, go for it. One caveat: The questions aren't inviting you to *solve* any of these problems at this point; they're just intended to identify and clarify them. Of course, if you *can* solve any of them, feel free! **But don't get into arguments about them.** If you're worried that you'll argue, don't try to compare your answers.

Whew!

Okay, that's a lot of soul-searching.

I'm guessing that the exercise you just completed was at least somewhat painful. Of course, I hope I'm wrong about that—but if going through those items left you feeling great about your relationship, you probably wouldn't be reading this book.

As I mentioned before, the idea of that exercise was to identify and help you understand your relationship in more detail. In Parts II and III of the book, we'll work on fixing it.

But to conclude the stock-taking process that Part I is all about, you'll need to face a scary question, which is the topic of Chapter 5.

Chapter 5

Should You Call It Quits?

Do You Wonder If You Should End It?

Many of you reading this have been wondering if you should end your relationship for a long time. It's been painful. What you've tried up to now hasn't worked. There are a host of possible reasons why you haven't ended it yet, but you've actively considered it. This chapter is for you.

Or maybe you are clear that you *don't* want to end the relationship—again, for any of a host of reasons. If that's you, you should still read this chapter. It will give you some useful perspectives. There's a risk, of course, that you might realize that you need to reconsider your thoughts about ending the relationship. But you might also find that your resolve to save it is strengthened.

Either way, the topics of this chapter will help prepare you for the work of Parts II and III. If you want to stay in the relationship, the work will be about learning the skills and fixing it so you both feel good about staying in it. If you decide you need to end the relationship, the work is about ending it in as humane a way as you can, so as to improve your life rather than making it worse. It's work either way—notwithstanding Paul Simon's "Fifty Ways to Leave Your Lover."

How Can You Decide?

There's no simple litmus test for deciding if you should work on fixing your relationship, or work on ending it. But here are some guidelines.

First, **if you're not physically safe in the relationship, get out.**

Assuming you're physically safe but unhappy, think about the problems you're having. You just went through a long process of identifying them in the last chapter.

For each problem, you'll decide if it's in one of two categories: (a) deal-breakers, or (b) growing pains.

Don't decide yet. Before you sort out your problems, let's talk about each of those categories. You might be surprised.

Deal-Breakers

Oddly enough, what makes a problem a deal-breaker isn't just about how painful it is. **Some very painful problems often turn out not to be deal-breakers, but growing pains. And some problems that don't seem to be that painful, at least not yet, can turn out to be deal-breakers.**

What, then, is a deal-breaker?

Bethany and Matt had been together for 12 years, since they each graduated from college. They loved each other, got along well, and enjoyed their life together. But soon after Bethany turned 30, she began to feel an intense need to have a baby. That feeling took her somewhat by surprise, especially because she and Matt had agreed that neither of them wanted to have kids. She tried hard to talk herself out of it.

But by the time they came to see me, when they were both 34, she couldn't deny it: she needed to become a mother. And however much Matt wanted to please her, he couldn't see himself as a father. Ever.

There's no compromise possible—you can't partly have a child. And there's no win-win possible either, unless one of them were to change their mind. Neither Bethany nor Matt could imagine doing that. Neither of their positions is wrong or pathological. They're just incompatible.

Deal-breaker.

Sam and Debbie had been a couple since high school, went to the same college, and moved in together after graduation. Then Debbie got deeply involved in her evangelical church. Sam wasn't religious—in fact, he was somewhat anti-religious—and couldn't accept raising children in Debbie's church. They realized, sadly, that they couldn't stay together.

Deal-breaker.

What makes a problem a deal-breaker is that there's no possible resolution that works if you stay together unless someone changes their deeply-held position. Here are some more classic deal-breakers:

- One of the partners is gay and the other is straight.
- Both partners insist on living near their extended families, which live thousands of miles apart.
- One partner has to live in the city and the other anywhere *but* the city.

Of course, even in those situations a couple could decide to stay together and try to find a work-around. The gay-straight couple could open the relationship to others sexually, or agree to remain celibate. The partners who need to live far apart to be near family or to be in an acceptable area could carry on a long-distance relationship, visiting each other as frequently as they can.

But the reason these situations are classic deal-breakers is that those solutions rarely work over the long haul.

The only thing that overcomes a deal-breaker is if one or the other partner genuinely changes their mind—in which case, it's no longer a deal-breaker. But there's a considerable risk of convincing yourself that you're really okay with something you're not. If you try to do that, you're courting resentment and bitterness. Not a great prospect for either stability or intimacy.

As I mentioned, a problem can be painful, even unacceptably painful, and still not be a deal-breaker. And there's no guarantee you'll decide to stay together even if there aren't any clear deal-breakers. If you're not sure—if you can see a possibility that the right kind of growth can resolve the problem—then it's not a deal-breaker.

But if you do identify a deal-breaker, at least you know what you'll need to do.

Growing Pains

If a problem isn't a deal-breaker, it's a growing pain. And if you're not sure, start with the assumption that it's a growing pain.

Remember Devon and Kara from Chapter 2? They're the couple that couldn't seem to stay together for more than a couple of months without separating, often after a nasty argument fueled by alcohol. Then they would get back together, and within a few weeks separate again. They had repeated the pattern for a year.

You could conclude that the repeated pattern itself indicates that they're not right for each other. That might be a sensible conclusion—indeed, lots of couples in that sort of situation ultimately split up.

But it's possible that they could learn some skills that would change the pattern. If they could each get better at emotional regulation—essentially, the skill of managing their anxiety without crossing over into freak-out territory—they might be able to turn things around and decide to stay together. It's not certain, but it's possible.

Which means this pattern isn't inherently a deal-breaker.

Why make the distinction? Why does it matter if we call this a growing pain, rather than a deal-breaker?

Because even if they ultimately split up, the skills they work on in an effort to grow past the problem will serve them well. They'll learn what they need to learn.

If they break up too soon—meaning before they've had a chance to learn from the situation—they'll miss that opportunity, and probably have to learn it in some future relationship.

And, of course, they could learn what they need to learn and decide to stay together. It's that possibility that distinguishes growing pains from deal-breakers. If it's possible to grow past the problem, it's not a deal-breaker.

Here are some more examples of problems that, no matter how painful, are growing pains rather than clear deal-breakers:

- One of you has cheated, which has precipitated an existential crisis in your relationship. As painful as that is, you might be able to get past the initial trauma, find each other again, and even come to appreciate the growth you've experienced together by working through the crisis. I've worked with dozens of spouses who were cheated on who told me early on that they never would have thought they'd try to save a

relationship with someone who cheated, but then went on to do just that and were glad they did.
- You're having painful problems in your sex life. You used to have a good sexual connection, but lately it's just not working. If you've had a good connection in the past, it can't be that your sexual orientations are fundamentally incompatible. So you might be able to learn more, address medical and relational issues, and develop new skills so as to have a satisfying sex life again.
- You're constantly fighting about anything and nothing; the slightest hint of disagreement seems to lead to arguments you later see as pointless. You might be able to get to the root of your mutual resentments, understand yourselves and each other, and come to respect and enjoy each other again.
- You disagree about how to raise the kids, or politics, or what sort of food to eat, or pretty much anything. In theory, you could develop new understandings of each other's points of view, and even come to appreciate the differences. Consider couples like Mary Matalin and James Carville (google them if you need to).

The Basic Guideline for Growing Pains

Recognizing that a problem is a growing pain rather than a deal-breaker doesn't mean you'll *certainly* be able to grow past it together. It just means you're seeing it as an opportunity to grow, together or separately. You don't know yet what's possible in practice. You just know that growing past the problem is at least possible in theory, and that growth will help you whether you stay together or not.

Which leads to my one basic guideline for handling growing pains.

If your problems are growing pains, don't break up too soon.

What's "too soon?" There's no fixed timeline—only you can determine that. But **if you're breaking up in a panic, because you can't stand not knowing whether you can fix it or not, you won't learn what you need to learn from the problem.** Remember the idea that tolerating anxiety is the essential skill for intimacy? This is a great example of when you need that skill. As I mentioned about Devon and Kara, if you don't learn it now, you'll probably have to learn it in a future relationship.

And when you do learn what you need to learn, you might find that your relationship is not only surviving, but is better than you ever imagined it could be. There's no guarantee of this—but I've seen it happen many times.

The Bias in this Approach

You may have noticed that this approach isn't neutral about the question of staying together or splitting up. It's biased in favor of staying together, or at least giving it your best shot.

I'm being explicit about this bias not because I disapprove of splitting up in all circumstances—indeed, I recognize that splitting up is often a necessary part of healing. I'm just saying it shouldn't be your go-to solution when things get hard.

That's why I'm saying that **a problem is a deal-breaker only if there's no logical possibility of resolving it sufficiently by learning or growth.** If you're not sure, assume it's a growing pain, because maybe you can fix it. I'm not saying you should never split up—just that you shouldn't leap to do so without learning what you need to learn.

Of course, you can disagree with that approach, and you wouldn't be alone. Many therapists and social media influencers will say, explicitly or not, "If you're not happy in a relationship, why stay in it?" This applies not only to marriages and couple relationships, but to other important relationships as well.

I'm not giving academic citations in this book, but if you'd like to see research on how often therapists make statements disparaging their clients' partners, with or without meeting them, and how this can affect relationships, google "Doherty relationship-undermining." Bill Doherty is a couples therapist who has written about the tendency of some therapists to promote splitting up, subtly or not. It's not universal, but it's very common for individual therapists to empathize with their clients in a way that supports their anger and resentments toward their partners, rather than inviting them to consider their own contributions to the problems they're having. And many couples therapists are quick to suggest divorce as a first-line solution for a couple in conflict.

That question, "If you're not happy in a relationship, why stay in it?" is understandable, but I think there are (at least) three good answers.

First, **people who successfully turn around troubled relationships are often enormously grateful**, not just for the positive outcome, but for what they learned going through the struggle. And even people who ultimately decide to split up are often grateful for what they learned by working on the relationship and making a considered decision, rather than giving in to panic.

Second, **couple relationships aren't only about the two people in the partnership**. Children, extended families, and wider communities are all affected. Marriage, in particular, is a recognition that your couple relationship isn't only about you and your partner. From that perspective, to heal a couple is to help heal wider systems as well. Many of the skills you learn in working on healing a couple in pain are applicable to healing communities in pain as well. To work in that way, with a commitment not only to our own individual happiness but to the well-being of all of us together, is fundamental to how I see my role.

The third answer is much simpler. **To hop from one relationship to another in hopes of finding the one that will**

make you happy won't work. You might have been trying that approach for a while. I'm not saying you can't get lucky and find someone well-suited to you. I'm just saying that if you haven't developed the skills of intimacy, you won't find happiness with someone else.

Now it's time to decide for yourself.

Deal-Breakers or Growing Pains?

Write down your impressions as you consider the questions below.

Do this task separately, not with your partner.

Consider each of the issues in your relationship that you identified in Chapter 4. As you might recall, there were 15 suggested areas to consider (including "other"). Many of them might not apply, or might be relatively unimportant, and you can ignore those for now. You'll be focusing on the areas that are causing you the most concern.

As you think about each problem, answer each of the following questions:

1. Is the problem a clear deal-breaker, or a growing pain? Remember, it's only a deal-breaker if there's no satisfactory solution possible unless someone changes their position, which neither partner is willing to do. If there's a possibility that one or both of you could learn new skills or otherwise grow past the problem, it's not a deal-breaker.

    As you answer question 1, note that you might not know for sure about some issues. For example, if you're having problems in your sex life, is it because your sexual orientations don't line up (potential deal-breaker), or because of relational or other issues you could try to fix (growing pain)? If you're not sure, it's not a deal-breaker.

2. If you *are* confronting a deal-breaker, how long have you been experiencing the issue? If it's been a while, which means you've

been living with the situation, what has changed to make you realize it's a deal-breaker? How have you been living with it up to now? If it's recent, how was it that you didn't experience it before?

3. If the problem is a growing pain, imagine a time in the future—maybe even the near future—when you start to see some signs of positive change. Maybe just hints at first. What might you notice that would indicate that the problem is starting to become less difficult? What skills will you have developed that have helped?

If you and your partner compared your answers when you did the exercise in Chapter 4, consider asking your partner to do the same now. If you're worried that this won't go well, don't do it.

What If You Can't (or Won't) Talk to Your Partner?

Of course, if you haven't wanted to involve your partner in the work you've been doing in this book, or if you've invited them but they declined, that itself could be an indicator of a problem in your relationship, particularly in the domain of intimacy.

But that particular problem definitely is in the category of growing pain, not deal-breaker. You might find, for example, that as you do the work in Part II it gets easier to talk with your partner about the issues you've identified. You might then want to go back over some of the tasks in Part I with your partner, and work together on identifying areas you need to work on.

Or you might find, as you develop the skills you'll learn in Part II, that you don't need to go back over Part I with your partner in any formal way. You might just be able to talk to your partner about whatever you need to.

In fact, to be able to do that—to talk with your partner about whatever either of you needs to—is one of the central goals of this work.

Now What?

If you haven't identified clear deal-breakers, you're ready for Part II of this book. You'll be working on honing the skills you need to be able to fix the problems you've identified. Growing pains are resolved by growth.

Even if you have identified a clear deal-breaker, I urge you to read on. You'll learn things that will help you going forward, whether it's in your current relationship or a future one. It's even possible that you might change your mind about a problem being a deal-breaker. Maybe there are ways to grow past the problem.

And if you've decided that you need to break up, there's a chapter about how to do that as humanely as possible. You'll notice that's the last chapter of Part III, because I'm inviting you to see splitting up as a last resort.

Part II

Learn the Skills

Chapter 6

How Do You Turn It Around?

What Do You Need to Learn?

Let's review what we've covered so far.

In Chapter 1, you assessed your relationship in terms of stability and intimacy. Chapter 2 then expanded on those concepts, and Chapter 3 described how passion can die in a couple when the demands of stability to avoid anxiety have the nasty side-effect of quashing intimacy. In Chapter 4, you took another look at your relationship in terms of stability and intimacy, and took a magnifying glass to a litany of potential problem areas, some of which might also have been areas of strength.

Then, in Chapter 5, you faced the question of whether you should work on staying together, or work on splitting up. We distinguished between deal-breakers and growing pains, and I urged you to err on the side of assuming a problem is a growing pain if there is any doubt. And even if you did conclude that you're confronting a clear deal-breaker, I urged you to work on the growing pains anyway, since what you learn from that work will benefit you either in your current relationship or in some future relationship.

At several junctures you were asked whether you wanted to invite your partner to do a lot of those same tasks and compare your answers. Whether or not you invited your partner to get involved, and whether or not they agreed, are also indicators of how your relationship is going. If you've been reluctant to talk to your partner about the work you're doing with this book, that itself indicates a barrier to intimacy.

So here you are. You've identified problem areas, and you're ready to work on them.

Where do you start? What skills do you need to develop? What do you need to learn?

Here's your answer.

What you need in your relationship is both stability and intimacy—so the skills you need are the skills that promote stability and intimacy.

And it turns out that the skills you need for stability are different from the skills you need for intimacy. In fact, there's some tension between the two skill sets. You need them both, but they're somewhat in conflict.

Which leads us to the key skill that makes all the others possible.

The Most Important Skill You'll Ever Learn

The key skill—the one that makes all the others possible—is to be able to accept contradictory truths simultaneously.

Let me put that more concretely. The key skill is to be able to simultaneously be grateful for and pissed at your partner. To be able to be annoyed by the dish left in the sink and delighted by having someone in your life who left it there. To be able to be disappointed when your partner won't have sex with you and appreciative of how alive your desire makes you feel. To be able to be irritated by your partner's cluelessness when they want to have sex with you when you're clearly not in the mood, and reassured that they desire and want to connect with you.

To be able to be both afraid and hopeful about the future of your relationship. To grieve loss and celebrate joy.

To recognize that your precious ideas and your partner's precious ideas might sometimes conflict, and yet both be true and correct in their own way. Which is to say, to have humility about your own views—you don't know everything.

To feel miles apart and still love each other. Recall the subtitle of this book.

If that subtitle is what brought you to this book, you're already practicing the key skill.

Without that key skill, the contradictions between what you need to do for stability and what you need to do for intimacy become unsurmountable barriers. The death spiral for passion we talked about in Chapter 3 is a symptom.

With that key skill…well, there are still no guarantees. But when you're able to accept the contradictions and work with them, amazing things can happen.

Gather Your Thoughts

Write down your impressions as you consider these questions. Do this by yourself first. If your partner is also doing these tasks, feel free to compare your answers.

1. Think about the times you've experienced mixed feelings about your relationship. Write down some of the contradictory feelings

you've had. (Note that this question assumes you've had some mixed feelings, because I can't imagine you haven't.) You might consider dichotomies such as appreciation/annoyance, hope/despair, anger/delight, desire/revulsion, or whatever comes to mind. Be as specific as you can about particular moments or events you associate with a given mix of feelings.

2. When you've experienced a mix of feelings, have you noticed it as such? For example, if you were feeling both annoyed and appreciative toward your partner, did you notice both feelings? Have you consciously remarked on it, at least to yourself? Have you found yourself lurching between extremes? Have you ever worried you must be crazy to have such contradictory feelings? Have you ever noticed the contradiction in your feelings and found some humor in it?

3. Have you noticed that your partner sometimes has mixed feelings? When your partner has shown irritation toward you, have you assumed that's all they're feeling toward you? Have you sometimes been able to recognize that irritation is only part of how they feel, and stay calm about it?

4. These questions have been presupposing that accepting contradictory feelings is important—crucial, even—to working on your relationship. Do you agree with that premise? If so, explain it in your own words. Why is it so important? What does that skill let you do, particularly when you're interacting with your partner? When you lack that skill—in other words, when you can't accept that your own feelings can be wildly mixed, and the same is true for your partner—what effects does that have?

In the section heading above I called this key skill the most important skill you'll ever learn. That's a large claim! I'm giving it that title because **the ability to accept, and even appreciate, contradictory truths is the basis for healing relationships**. And the converse, the insistence that only one understanding of a situation can be true, and that other understandings are necessarily false, ultimately destroys both intimacy and stability.

We'll explore why I think that skill is so important, and what you can do to develop it, in Chapter 7. For now, let's consider the skill sets you need for stability and for intimacy, and why they're not the same.

The Skills of Stability

You might recall from Chapter 2 that stability skills are all about keeping the anxiety level as low as possible—essentially, acting in ways that aren't alarming to either your partner or yourself.

This means being **reliable, responsible, and accountable**.

Reliable means that you show up when you say you will, and do what you say you're going to do. **Responsible** means that you consider the consequences of your choices, anticipate what needs to be done and act on it, and carry your share of the load. **Accountable** means that you're willing to listen if your partner raises a concern about you, re-evaluate your behavior, and find ways to make amends if you've done wrong.

Boring, right?

Exactly. Stability is boring. Nobody wants to read a novel about characters who are unerringly reliable, responsible, and accountable. (There's no song titled "Call Me Responsible" either.)

Fortunately, none of us is *unerringly* reliable, responsible, or accountable. Most of us blow it frequently enough to supply some non-boring episodes. No need to manufacture these—they'll happen on their own.

Perfection is neither possible nor desirable. But if you want your relationship to survive, you need to be *mostly* reliable, responsible, and accountable.

Gather Your Thoughts

Write down your impressions as you consider these questions. Work on them yourself first. Then feel free to discuss them with your partner.

1. How would you rate yourself in terms of reliability, responsibility, and accountability? One way to think about this is to consider whether you'd like to be your own partner in forming a stable life. Could you count on yourself to show up reliably? Could you trust that you'd think ahead about the consequences of your actions, and would carry your share of the load? Would you be open to hearing a complaint or request? If you were considering someone exactly like yourself as a potential partner in creating a stable relationship, would you be enthusiastic, head for the hills, or something in between?
2. Think about how your partner might view *your* stability skills. Do you think they'd agree with your self-assessment? How might they agree or disagree with you about your stability skills? Note that I'm not asking (yet) about your partner's stability skills.
3. Staying with your own stability skills (or lack thereof), think about some moments where you've been less than great. Do you think of those moments as exceptions, or do you see yourself as a perennial screwup, or something in between?
4. If you do see yourself as something of a screwup, what do you attribute that to? Was it a difficult childhood, or unprocessed trauma, or are you just a bad person? (You're not a bad person, but do you think you are?)
5. If you haven't been doing well in terms of stability skills, do you believe it's possible to do better—that is, to learn and grow in a way that will help you be a better partner? (If you don't believe that's possible, keep reading. By the end of this book I hope you'll change your mind!) What have you tried?
6. Think back some number of years—say, half of your life since you were 20. (So if you're 30, think back about five years, and if you're 60, think back about 20 years.) How would you compare

your level of stability skills now to then? How would you account for the changes?
7. Now consider your partner's reliability, responsibility, and accountability. How would you describe them? Of course, neither of you is perfect in those areas, but what are the relative strengths and weaknesses you've noticed?
8. Thinking about both yourself and your partner, how do your respective strengths and weaknesses affect each other? For example, is one of you hyper-responsible and the other hyper-irresponsible? Do you appreciate the ways each of you compensates for the other's relative weaknesses, or resent them, or some combination?

Working on Stability Skills

I noted in Chapter 2 that the skills we've just been talking about are essentially markers of maturity and character.

Which means that **to improve your stability skills, you need to grow up and be a mensch** (that's a Yiddish word for a person of character). There's your basic challenge.

I speculated earlier that you're probably pretty good at stability skills. If so, you might have found the questions above mostly reassuring, at least about yourself. You might have identified some areas of improvement (yes, you really should get better at texting your partner to tell them when you'll be later than expected), but you're mostly okay in terms of stability. Your big challenges will be about intimacy.

But I recognize that some of you may have come through the questions above and concluded, "Wow—I really suck as a partner." In fact, many of the people I've worked with have been assuming that for years. If you've had multiple relationships that have been unstable thrill rides that eventually go off the track, you might well have recognized that the common denominator is you.

Indeed, the problem might well be that, so far, you *do* suck as a partner.

If that's you, your first challenge will be to imagine that you can change that. Until you recognize that you're capable of being a good partner, your efforts to improve will continue to fail. The problem isn't that you don't know what to do. The problem is that you believe you're unable to grow.

That's not a cognitive problem, or even an emotional problem. It's a spiritual problem. (If you're not religious, don't worry—you don't have to be religious to work on a spiritual problem.) We'll be working on it in Chapter 7. For now, I invite you to at least imagine that you're capable of learning and growth. I'm confident you can do that, or you wouldn't have made it this far in the book.

Whether or not you need to work on stability skills, working on intimacy skills will be the main event.

The Skills of Intimacy

I noted above that the skills of stability are boring. Well, the skills of intimacy certainly aren't boring.

They're terrifying.

Recall what I mean by intimacy: Intimacy for a couple is when you're each present and honest with yourself and each other.

To be present and honest with yourself implies that you're able to feel what you feel and think what you think and say what you want to say without either shutting down or panicking. To be present and honest with your partner means all of that, plus being able to hear your partner say things you may or may not want to hear, without shutting down or panicking.

Of course, you don't *always* face anxiety when you're in an intimate encounter. Sometimes everything just clicks, and intimacy feels effortless. You might recall times like that early in your relationship, when it seemed that this amazing person who became your partner was so easy to be with. You could talk for hours, or just sit together and enjoy a lovely setting, or have mind-blowing sex. When you think of those times now, you're probably not remembering high anxiety.

But **intimacy isn't only about pleasant encounters**. Sometimes what you need to be honest about is something you're pretty sure your partner isn't going to receive well. And if trying to be honest has led to painful blowups or freezes, you'll become that much more afraid to be honest in the future.

Which leads to the death spiral we described in Chapter 3.

As we noted in Chapter 2, the essential skill for intimacy is to tolerate anxiety, rather than avoiding it. That's the way out of the death spiral—which means that's the basic skill you'll need to improve. The other skills of intimacy that we'll work on in specific contexts in later chapters all derive from that basic skill.

Gather Your Thoughts

Write down your impressions as you consider these questions. Work on them yourself first. Then feel free to discuss them with your partner.

1. If something is bothering you, how willing are you to talk to your partner about it? What if what's bothering you is something your partner is or isn't doing? Are there some topics that you're particularly reluctant to bring up with your partner? Are there some topics that feel easy to bring up? Can you talk about finances? Sex? Kid issues? In-laws?
2. Think back to the early days of your relationship. How easy was it for you to talk with your partner about things that might be bothering you? Has that sense of ease changed over time? Do you remember specific incidents that seemed to be turning points?

3. If you're worried about bringing up something with your partner, have you talked to them about your worry? If so, how did that go?
4. Have there been times when you've taken a risk and brought up something with your partner even though you're worried about how it will go? Think of some specific instances. If it went generally well, what did you do that helped? If it went generally badly, what went wrong? What might either of you have done differently?
5. How willing does your partner seem to be to bring up something with you? Has your partner talked to you about difficulties bringing up certain topics with you? If so, how did it go?
6. If your partner told you they are often afraid to bring up some issues with you, would you be surprised? Why might they worry about your reaction?

As we've noted, **the skills of intimacy are all based on your ability and willingness to tolerate anxiety, rather than avoiding it.** And the anxiety you need to tolerate isn't crazy or unrealistic. You can't talk yourself out of it. You'll need to learn to tolerate it.

Stability Skills and Intimacy Skills Are (Partly) in Conflict

Remember my assertion earlier in this chapter about the most important skill you'll ever learn? I said that the key skill—the one that makes all the others possible—is to be able to accept contradictory truths simultaneously.

To have both stability and intimacy in your relationship requires skill sets that are inherently in conflict, but you need them both.

For stability, you need to be reliable, responsible, and accountable—the boring trifecta. That means you're essentially predictable in how you act. You're steady, sensible, and in control of your emotions.

For intimacy, you need to be willing to risk being honest about how you feel, even if that upsets your partner. You need to let yourself know about your fantasies, your desires, your hopes, your fears, your uncertainties, and be willing to share them with your partner. And many of those hopes and fears are changing from year to year and moment to moment. You're *not* always steady, sensible, and in control of your emotions.

You need both sets of skills—even when they conflict.

In Chapter 7, we'll focus on developing the mindset that will let you accept the contradictions, hone your skills, and apply them to your relationship. But first, let's consider what *doesn't* work.

Communication Tools Don't Help

Yes, you want to get on with what *does* help.

But I'm guessing you've been trying to find solutions for a while. You may have tried some of the communication approaches I'm about to talk about—and you're here because they didn't work. Or you've heard about these and are thinking you might want to try them. Either way, this section will help you understand why these approaches don't work, and point you towards what will. If you've been expecting this book to teach you communication techniques, here's why it won't.

I wrote a book about this, called *It's Not About Communication!* (Go buy it and read it—I'll wait here!) Here's the executive summary.

Most of the couples who come to consult me tell me, in the first session, that they need to communicate better. You might feel the same way. Whenever you and your partner try to talk about anything more emotional than "please pass the salt," you seem to end up in a screaming match, deep freeze, or some combination. Wouldn't it help to learn some techniques to improve communication?

If you and your partner were actually having trouble communicating, that would be a good idea. But you're almost certainly not.

We've already ruled out the possibility that you or your partner are experiencing psychosis, which would indeed cause communication problems. You're not psychotic, but maybe you or your partner are on the autistic spectrum, and aren't skilled at identifying other people's emotions, which would also cause communication problems. It's even possible that you and your partner do not speak the same language—I mean literally, like one of you speaks only English and other hardly any English—which of course causes communication problems.

If one of those situations applies, maybe you *do* have trouble communicating.

But couples therapy won't solve any of those issues; you'd need individual mental health treatment, or skills training in how to recognize emotions, or language classes and practice.

Assuming none of those situations apply to you, you don't need help communicating. You already communicate effectively.

The problem isn't *how* you're communicating. It's *what* you're communicating.

You're reading this because you're struggling in your relationship. So what you've been communicating—very effectively—reflects those struggles. You and your partner might be communicating anger, mistrust, contempt, condescension, fear, and all sorts of other painful messages. No communication techniques will hide those messages.

There are shelves full of books and terabytes of websites and thousands of therapists who will happily teach you to use I-messages, active listening, nonviolent communication, and various other techniques. Maybe you've tried them. And if they worked for you, great—although the fact that you're reading this suggests otherwise.

Yes, there is research that couples who are happy with each other tend to communicate in ways that look like they're following some of those communication rules, albeit informally. Check out John Gottman's research, for example.

But those couples aren't happy because they're following the rules. They're following the rules because they're happy. In fact, they don't need the rules. And if those happy couples tried to apply those rules formally, they'd find them cumbersome and silly.

If you're not one of those happy couples—if you've been communicating mostly pain to each other—then the techniques won't do you any good. **You can be every bit as cold or contemptuous with an I-message as you can with a you-message.**

Worse, when you're in a panic you won't be able to apply the techniques, because the part of your brain that can apply them is offline. And when you're not in a panic, the techniques just provide something else to argue about, and reinforce how miserable you are with each other.

We've been talking about stability and intimacy. Communication techniques are entirely about stability—they're ways of trying to avoid anxiety by structuring how you communicate. But they do so to the detriment of intimacy. Can you imagine carefully crafting your language when you're in the midst of great sex? Or when you're sharing moments of deep grief?

You don't need to learn communication techniques. You need to develop the skills of intimacy, not just stability. And that means learning to tolerate and manage the inevitable anxiety that comes with risking honesty with yourself and your partner.

Then What Will Work?

As we've said, you need to develop the skill of tolerating anxiety rather than avoiding it. That means cultivating a particular mindset, which is the topic of Chapter 7.

Gather Your Thoughts

Write down your impressions as you consider these questions. Work on them yourself first. Then feel free to discuss them with your partner.

1. Have you tried any of the communication techniques I mentioned—I-statements, active listening, nonviolent communication, or others? If so, how did it go? Did they help? (Just because I said they don't help doesn't mean I'm right.) If they helped, what about using the technique helped?
2. Many people I've worked with tell me that they plan carefully before they bring something up with their partner that might be controversial or otherwise upsetting. It's akin to "walking on eggshells." They'll try to gauge their partner's mood and receptivity, and carefully couch what they're bringing up in language they hope will make it easier to hear. Does that description sound familiar to you? If so, why would you feel the need to plan? How often does it work, in the sense that you emerge from the conversation feeling relieved? When it hasn't worked, why do you think it hasn't?
3. Do you think your partner sometimes walks on eggshells with you? Would they have reason to do so?
4. I mentioned above that developing the skill of tolerating anxiety—which is the chief skill you need for intimacy—involves cultivating a particular mindset. Before you go into Chapter 7, think about what that might mean. "Mindset" means a general orientation to seeing the world. What general beliefs and understandings about living might help you face anxiety and risk

honesty with your partner? You might come up with different ideas than I do—don't worry about getting it "right."

Chapter 7

What is Faith?

Why Faith?

I invited you at the end of Chapter 6 to think about what mindset you would need to be able to tolerate the anxiety of intimacy. My answer to that question is faith.

You're looking for solutions. This isn't a philosophy book. Why am I telling you about faith?

As you might have surmised, I'm telling you about it because faith is the key to being able to find solutions. **So learning about faith, and how to practice it as a skill, underpins everything else you'll be doing in this workbook.** You need this chapter.

I realize that the word "faith" might be problematic for some of you. And even if you're comfortable with the word, you might be understanding it in a way that is very different from what I mean.

I've written elsewhere about why I use the word faith to describe the mindset you need for intimacy, even at the risk of confusing it with religion. (Another book of mine to rush out and buy is *Betrayal and Forgiveness*, where I go into a lot of detail about that.) For now, if the word gets in your way, bear with me.

When I use the word faith, this is what I mean:

Faith is when you accept that reality is right to be what it is.

I can't sell you on that idea if you don't agree. There's no way to *prove* that reality is right to be what it is.

We can argue about *what* reality is—what the facts are—and test what we think using the tools of science. But faith as I define it isn't an assertion about the facts. Rather, **faith is an attitude, a value judgement, a mindset.** It's not *only* accepting reality for what it is, though that's part of it (dealing with life on life's terms, as people in 12-step programs sometimes say). Faith is accepting that reality, whatever it is, is *right* to be that way.

If I feel that reality is right to be what it is, I'm saying it's essentially good, even though I'm well aware that reality includes the whole range of good and evil, pleasurable and painful, inspiring and horrifying. It's recognizing that I can't possibly understand it all, or have all the answers. But even that unavoidable uncertainty is right to be that way.

Real life isn't certain. If faith entails accepting real life, claiming certainty is the opposite of faith.

This isn't just semantics. It has real effects.

Have you been tempted to call your partner, or yourself, a narcissist or borderline or some other disordered personality based on a checklist? Have you used Myers-Briggs or enneagram types, or astrological charts, or attachment styles, or any other sort of classification scheme, with the expectation that you'll understand your problems with your partner if you come up with the right labels?

It's not that those techniques have no value. It's just that they never tell the whole story. And when you're talking about relationships, they don't tell nearly as much of the story as the people who sell the techniques claim.

Lots of therapists and websites and support groups will help you find support for those ideas, and proceed to tell you what you can expect based on those labels. If you think labeling someone, or yourself, will explain everything, you've fallen prey to fundamentalism—which is the opposite of faith as I'm describing it. (Notice that secular fundamentalism can be just as limiting as religious fundamentalism.)

Remember when I claimed that the ability to accept contradictory truths is the most important skill you'll ever learn? **Life is full of contradictory truths—not about *facts*, but about *meaning*.** We might have different opinions about facts, but even when we agree on facts we can have very different understandings of what those facts imply for how we should live.

To have faith means not merely to accept that reality, but to embrace it. **It's *right* that we can't always find a single, irrefutable understanding of life's problems.** It's *right* that different people—different sane, intelligent, decent people—come up with opposite answers to difficult questions.

That doesn't mean you can't have your own opinions, even firmly held opinions. There are values that I would give my life to uphold, and maybe you would too. But **an attitude of faith is a check on the arrogance of certainty.** I may well fight for what's important to me, but I need to accept that my judgments are fallible. Which means I need to be open to the possibility that I might learn from someone else's contrary ideas. Or even from someone else's bad behavior.

That check on the arrogance of certainty is especially important when you're in conflict with your partner.

Faith and Intimacy

Back in Chapter 2, I stated what I called the central thesis of this book:

The essential skill for intimacy is tolerating anxiety, rather than avoiding it.

You've already speculated (in the last prompt in Chapter 6) about what might make tolerating anxiety possible. What sort of mindset lets you be honest with your partner, and listen to your partner's honesty, without crossing over into panic?

You could say it's courage, but that's just another word for acting in the face of fear. What is it about your beliefs, feelings, or understandings that lets you have the courage to take the risk?

It's faith. **Faith is what lets people risk intimacy.**

Gather Your Thoughts

Consider the situations below labeled A through H, about a couple called Chris and Alex. Note that their genders are deliberately indeterminate, so you can imagine whatever combination works for you. We're assuming that both Chris and Alex are essentially sane, intelligent, and good at heart (recall those are the same things I'm assuming about you and your partner.)

I'm guessing you might be familiar with some of these situations, but if not just imagine yourself in a similar situation.

For each situation, consider the sets of questions labeled 1 and 2 (below, after the situations).

Here are the situations:

A. Chris is thinking about proposing a move together to another part of the country.

B. Chris has thought of suggesting something to try sexually (a sex toy, watching porn together, oral, anal, a threesome, whatever), but isn't sure how or whether to bring it up with Alex.
C. Chris has developed serious doubts about the religion the two of them have practiced together for years.
D. Chris's ex texted Chris, and they carried on a text conversation, even though Chris knows Alex doesn't want them to communicate.
E. Chris was put on probation on the job after failing to meet standards, and hasn't told Alex.
F. Chris has run up expenses on a credit card and needs to ask Alex for money to pay it down.
G. Chris agreed to stop drinking, but has been secretly drinking when away from Alex.
H. Chris had a one-night stand with someone on a business trip, and has just returned home.

Here are the questions to consider for each situation:

1. Imagine you're Chris. Why might you be worried about discussing the situation with Alex? What reactions are you afraid of? What has stopped you from talking about it up to now? Are your worries crazy, or do you understand why you're worried?
2. Now switch roles and imagine being Alex. Would you understand why Chris was reluctant to bring up the situation with you? Would Chris's reluctance be crazy, or understandable?

Now **go through the situations, and write down your impressions as you consider the two sets of questions for each situation.**

Some more questions to consider:

Having imagined yourself as Chris, and then as Alex, how do you feel about each of them? How hard was it for you to imagine being in their roles in each situation?

And one more question, regarding the situation labeled H, where Chris had a one-night stand. Imagine you were Alex, and Chris has told you about the cheating. Let's give you a week or two to get past the initial shock. In fact, let's say you and Chris are in your first couples therapy session.

You might not know if you want to try to stay together, but let's assume for now that you at least want to consider the possibility of staying together.

Here's the question: What do you want to know from Chris?

Give it some thought, and **write down your impressions**.

Faith and Your Relationship

Why did I just lead you through that exercise?

Aside from the possibility that you might be in some similar situations yourself, I hope what you just did gave you some practice with a mindset of faith.

As you were imagining yourself in Chris's or Alex's shoes, were you able to see each situation from both sides? Were you able to understand how someone who is essentially sane, decent, and intelligent could still end up in the situation? That doesn't require that you condone what Chris was doing in those situations that involved violating important values. It just means that you could see how a decent person could be vulnerable to making some bad decisions.

Let's revisit the last question from the exercise above. You found out that Chris has cheated on you, and a couple of weeks later you're starting couples therapy. What do you want to know from Chris?

How you answer that question can be quite revealing.

Let's meet two couples I've worked with who were in that same situation.

When Charles and Alicia first came to see me, Charles had confessed to Alicia about his one-night stand on a business trip a couple of weeks before. Charles had apologized repeatedly, and Alicia alternated between anger and desperation. They both said they wanted to save their marriage.

Both Alicia and Charles wanted their relationship to go back to how it was before the business trip. They were fine, they said—if Charles hadn't done that stupid thing they wouldn't need therapy.

Alicia was clear: Charles was on probation with her. He needed to let her monitor his phone, report his whereabouts to her, and reassure her whenever she wanted it. As for couples therapy, it was about setting up rules for Charles to follow to prevent him from cheating again. Any attempt to "explain" why he cheated was just making excuses for inexcusable behavior. Charles just wanted Alicia to accept his apology and his assurance that he would never do it again. He hoped eventually she'd stop needing constant reassurance and they could go on as before.

Chip and Aliza had a very similar story: Chip had told Aliza about his one-night stand a couple of weeks before their first session. Chip felt deeply remorseful, and Aliza was hurt and angry.

But there was one crucial difference in how Chip and Aliza approached therapy, compared to Charles and Alicia.

Both Aliza and Chip recognized from the outset that there's no way to go back to how their relationship was before—in fact, that going back was not only impossible, but would not even be a good idea if it were possible.

As Aliza put it, "I know Chip isn't a horrible person. I know he's not crazy. I love him, and I believe him when he says he loves me. So I'm going to have to understand what happened, and I need to know he understands what happened. That's the only way I can trust him again." Chip agreed, and added, "I can't just write it off as a momentary lapse. I wish I could. But I need to understand it myself. I wouldn't believe Aliza if she said she trusted me, unless we both understood what happened."

Aliza and Chip approached therapy realizing that they would need to explore the meaning of what happened, rather than rejecting it as meaningless.

In other words, they had a mindset of faith.

As painful as it was, Aliza and Chip knew they needed to work with what happened and learn from it. Alicia and Charles, in contrast, just wanted reality to go away.

Again, let's revisit the last question from the exercise in the last section, and apply it to the two couples we just met. What did Alicia want to know from Charles? What did Aliza want to know from Chip?

Alicia just wanted to know that Charles wouldn't do it again. She didn't want to hear why he thought he did it, or what was happening in their relationship that might have made him vulnerable to that choice. She just wanted rules and procedures that would keep it from happening again.

Aliza wanted to understand what had happened: what Chris was thinking and feeling that led him to stray, what part they each had in the state of their relationship that might have contributed, and whatever else might help them move forward, together or separately.

The problems you've been having in your relationship—the ones that led you to this book—won't be solved by wishing them away, or attributing them to some diagnostic label. You'll need to accept what has happened, and learn from it.

That's what I mean by a mindset of faith.

How Do You Acquire Faith?

If faith is so important, how do you get it?

If faith were a set of facts, you could learn them by studying the facts. But **faith isn't a set of facts.** As I said, a mindset of faith isn't an assertion that certain things are true. Rather, **faith is an attitude** that reality, whatever it is, is basically good, even when it's painful and hard to understand. To live with faith is to believe that the whole business is worth the effort. It's the opposite of despair.

I can't convince you that faith is correct, because faith is no more correct (or incorrect) than any other attitude. But I do hope to convince you that faith is a good way to live. More specifically, I hope to convince you that **faith is the one skill that facilitates all the other ones you'll need to develop to deal with the problems you're having in your relationship.**

Faith is a *skill*. You learn it like you learn any skill: by practicing it. Of course, you'll only practice it if you feel it's worth practicing. This means you need to choose a mindset of faith.

You don't *acquire* faith. You *choose* it.

What If You're Depressed?

Being clinically depressed is basically the absence of faith, or more accurately, a severely reduced ability to practice the attitude of faith.

That isn't the definition of depression you'll find in the diagnostic manual. But I think it's a useful way of describing it.

If you're depressed, you don't perceive that choosing faith is an option, any more than someone with a severed spinal cord can perceive that walking without assistance is an option.

Each of those situations involves disability. But someone with a spinal cord injury can learn to accept the new reality, adapt to the changes, and get on with living. In other words, you can have a spinal cord injury and deal with it with a mindset of faith.

What makes depression so pernicious is that it robs you of the very ability to adapt to it. It's a self-reinforcing disability.

You're already showing faith by doing this workbook. You wouldn't be doing this if you didn't believe that you can do something to improve your situation. That itself is an attitude of faith.

So even though you might be sad about your situation, and even if you've received a diagnosis of depression, the fact that you've come this far implies you're still able to see possibilities. You're still able to at least consider practicing faith.

Yes, keep taking your antidepressant medication, and keep your therapy appointments, and keep up your behavioral activation activities, and keep doing your mindfulness practices, and whatever else you find helpful. But **you don't need to wait to choose faith.**

Just as depression is self-reinforcing, so is a practice of faith.

How Do You Practice Faith?

You can't get faith out of a book (even this one). You have to practice it. How do you do that?

You start by choosing to do it. Then you find teachers, and see what they do. Faith is contagious.

The Talmud (Berakhot 62a) presents a series of vignettes about three different rabbis. Each of the first two describes a rabbi following his esteemed teacher into the outhouse to observe (among other things) how he wipes himself. The third describes a rabbi who hides under his esteemed teacher's bed to observe how he makes love with his wife. Each of the three vignettes concludes with the rabbi being asked how he could do something so impertinent. Each of them replies, "It is Torah, and I must learn."

Okay, I don't recommend learning to practice faith as the rabbis in those stories did. But you can do something similar (leaving out the creepy stalking parts).

First, you need to identify some teachers who exemplify a mindset of faith. Then spend time with them. You'll learn what living with faith entails, not by talking about it, but by experiencing it.

Find Teachers

How do you find teachers who can show you how to practice faith?

Start with the ones you might expect. If you're involved in a religious community, consider the clergy you know: pastors, priests, rabbis, imams, elders, spiritual leaders. Or in secular contexts: therapists, coaches, support groups, sponsors.

Unfortunately, not all clergy, professionals, or friends will be good exemplars of faith. How can you tell when you're with someone who is manifesting faith?

You can tell because when you're with them, you sense acceptance, respect, humility, reverence, wonder, appreciation, gratitude. These are attitudes of faith. The more you experience them, the more you open your heart and mind to them, the more you acquire those attitudes yourself.

When you learn to recognize those attitudes, you'll start to find them all over the place. Mentors, friends, bartenders, AA sponsors, parents, newborn babies, dogs, horses—all can teach you faith.

Religious clergy can offer the experience of faith, if they're not too stuck on their own righteousness. Beware of fundamentalist approaches that claim certainty, ignore complexity, and enforce rigid rules and interpretations. Those are not attitudes of faith, but of arrogance.

Therapists can also offer the experience of faith, and can even talk about it if they're not too freaked out about the concept themselves. Just as with religion, beware of fundamentalist approaches in therapy, which reduce you to a diagnosis or archetype or case study.

Gather Your Thoughts

Write down your impressions as you consider these questions:

1. How do you understand the idea of faith? How does faith fit in your life? Your understanding may be different from mine, especially if you associate faith with belief in God or a particular religion. How does your understanding of faith overlap with what I've been telling you about? How does it differ?
2. I've claimed that a mindset of faith as I describe it is the key to developing the skills you need to work on your relationship. Try to explain what I mean by that in your own words. If you can, find someone—it could be your partner or a friend—and talk about it with them. If you did that, what did you learn about their understanding of faith? How did that conversation affect your own relationship to faith?
3. Who in your life exemplifies faith? Who are your teachers, formally or informally? When I noted in passing that even newborn babies, dogs, and horses can be teachers of faith, did that resonate for you?
4. How might you actively practice those attitudes of faith that I described—acceptance, respect, humility, reverence, wonder, appreciation, gratitude? I'm saying that spending time with teachers who show those attitudes, especially when you're open to noticing them, will bring them out in you. Does that seem plausible? Have you had experiences like that?
5. Have you worked with professional helpers such as clergy, coaches, or therapists? If so, how helpful was it? If it was helpful, what helped? If it wasn't helpful, what got in the way? When you think about your work with those helpers, to what extent do you recall experiences of those attitudes of faith I listed above?
6. Have you and your partner ever worked together with a couples therapist or coach or clergyperson? If so, how did it go? If not,

have you wanted to, but your partner has resisted? Or has your partner wanted to, but you've resisted? If either of you has resisted, why? What concerns have stopped you or your partner? What might you be worried about that could happen in couples work? Are your worries crazy? (Recall that I'm assuming that neither of you is crazy.)

Chapter 8

Should You Try Couples Therapy?

Is Couples Therapy the Answer?

As you know, you're reading a book by a couples therapist. So you might think I'd automatically recommend couples therapy as at least worth a try.

Oddly enough, **I don't automatically recommend couples therapy.** In some situations, couples therapy is a bad idea. In other situations, couples therapy might be just what you need—but only if you're able to use it effectively, and only if the therapist is offering something helpful rather than useless or worse.

Let's cover the contraindications first, and then consider what might make couples therapy a good next step.

When You Shouldn't Do Couples Therapy

Couples therapy requires that you be able to handle potentially painful conversations without freaking out. In other words, you need to tolerate the anxiety of intimate conversations.

If you're not physically safe if your partner is upset—or vice versa—couples therapy is dangerous. If you're not physically safe in your relationship, you don't need couples therapy. Get out and get safe.

Assuming physical safety isn't a concern, you could try couples therapy. That will require that your partner agree to do it—we'll talk about that in Chapter 8. But just agreeing to try it doesn't guarantee that it will do you any good.

Here are some situations when you should *not* do couples therapy.

You're having an affair, and you're don't intend to tell your partner about it. This isn't all that unusual at the beginning of couples therapy. The only times I find out about it, of course, are when the partner having the affair comes clean. Sometimes, surprisingly, a couple can recover from this, especially if the partner comes clean early in the work. But it's not a good bet. **If you don't intend to be honest, don't do couples therapy.** (This is a moment where my old inner statistician reminds me that I don't know about the people in this situation who *didn't* come clean and just lied about it the whole time I worked with them. I suppose it's possible that I helped some of those couples. But I doubt it.)

You're planning on suing your partner for full custody of the children, and want to use couples therapy to gather evidence to support your case. To do couples therapy in this situation is deceptive. See the comment above about honesty. I routinely refuse to work with couples who are actively pitted against each other in a court case. If you're looking for dirt on your partner to use against them, hire an investigator. Or just don't.

You're not at physical risk, but your partner controls your finances, and you fear being left without resources if your partner gets angry enough. This situation is similar to being at physical risk, but it admits of a possible preliminary step that might make couples therapy possible. If you can arrange to have some financial safety net—some emergency funds you'll have access to even if your partner is in full jerk mode—then you might find couples therapy useful. I've seen situations where the financially vulnerable partner feels at risk even though the financially powerful partner *hasn't* been a jerk about it. When couples in that situation arrange for a safety net for the vulnerable partner, they're often *both* relieved, and can enter couples therapy productively.

You've been mandated by a court to do couples therapy. Well, this is a double-bind. The court has ordered couples therapy in hopes that the two of you will solve some of the issues you're dealing with in court. But the very fact that it's court-ordered usually makes the therapy performative rather than genuine, so those issues don't get solved. As I noted above, I won't work with couples in this situation. Mediation might be more useful, because it's about coming to a workable agreement—in other words, mediation is about stability, not intimacy.

Gather Your Thoughts

Write down your impressions as you consider these questions:

1. Are you physically safe with your partner? Is your partner physically safe with you? If not, couples therapy isn't what you need.
2. Are you keeping a significant secret from your partner—significant in the sense that if they knew it, it would cause them distress and call into question whether you can be trusted? If so, do you plan to tell your partner about it? If not, are you concerned that your partner is keeping a significant secret from you?

3. Are you financially vulnerable in the sense that I described above? Or is your partner financially vulnerable in that sense? Have you talked about it with each other?

When Couples Therapy Might Help

Assuming you're not in the situations I described in the previous section, couples therapy might help you, with two provisos: (1) you and your partner are able to use it effectively, and (2) the therapist is offering something useful.

Regarding the first proviso, you won't be surprised by what I think you need to be able to use couples therapy effectively.

You need faith.

Reread Chapter 7 if you need to. Recall that faith, as I use the term, means accepting that reality is right to be what it is.

You need to approach couples therapy recognizing that whatever is going on, you need to work with it, not wish it away. That's the "accepting reality" part of faith. And you need to recognize that whatever is going on isn't just crazy or evil or stupid, and neither are you or your partner. It's meaningful, even if you don't understand it. That's the "accepting that reality is *right*" part of faith.

Regarding the second proviso, about what the therapist is offering, you also won't be surprised by what I think. **The therapist also needs faith.**

What does it mean for the therapist to act with faith? Pretty much what I just said it means for you. The therapist needs to start with the assumption that you're both essentially sane, intelligent, and good at heart. (Just as I assumed about you, the reader.) And the therapist needs to seek meaning with you, rather than pathologize you or your situation.

Unfortunately, there's no simple way to find that kind of therapist. You can't tell from their credentials or training, because faith isn't specific to particular schools of thought. You pretty much need to give someone a try and see if they're a good fit. If you're feeling respected, and the therapist doesn't claim to know all the answers, you're probably in good hands, but ultimately you and your partner will have to decide if it's helping or not.

Before you consider finding a therapist, you'll need to consider if you even want to try couples therapy. And if you do, you'll need to invite your partner to join you—even if they might resist the idea. That's the topic of Chapter 9.

Gather Your Thoughts

Write down your impressions as you consider these questions:

1. Have you tried couples therapy, either with your current partner or a previous partner? If so, how did it go?
2. If you've tried couples therapy before and it was helpful, what seemed to be the most helpful aspects?
3. If you've tried couples therapy before and it wasn't particularly helpful, what seemed to get in the way?
4. Whether or not you've tried couples therapy before, do you think it could be helpful now? What are the pros and cons as you see them?
5. If you think couples therapy might be helpful, have you suggested it to your partner? If not, why not? If so, how did it go?
6. If you suggested couples therapy to your partner and they declined or expressed doubts, what did they say concerned them? How do you understand why they're resisting the idea? If you've tried to convince them, how did that go?

Chapter 9

Will Your Partner Try Couples Therapy with You?

How to Get Your Reluctant Partner to Try Couples Therapy

Throughout this book I've made some educated guesses about you, the reader. I've guessed—more than guessed, assumed—that you're sane, intelligent, and good at heart. I've guessed that you're pretty good at the skills of stability, and that the skills you most need to work on are related more to intimacy.

Here's another guess. **I'm guessing that you've seriously considered couples therapy.** (If you're actually in couples therapy with your partner now, you might still find this chapter helpful, because even when you're in therapy one of you might still be somewhat reluctant to continue.)

As with all the other guesses, I could be wrong about this one. Maybe you're doing this workbook in hopes of not needing couples therapy—and it could indeed turn out that way.

But if you've turned to a book like this, you're seeking solutions to painful problems. To make it this far, you've already demonstrated that you're willing to consider trying things you haven't tried, even if those things are scary. Couples therapy is one of those things.

You've probably given it some thought. But would your partner agree if you proposed trying couples therapy? Of course, I just invited you to think about that at the end of Chapter 8.

My guess about this one is that you *aren't* sure that your partner would agree if you proposed couples therapy. One of you resists the idea, and it's probably your partner. And maybe you've been trying to figure out how to get them to change their mind.

And if my guess is wrong, and you're resisting the idea yourself, keep reading, because the same approach that might help your partner open up to the possibility can work for you as well.

Let's meet another couple.

When I met them, Gina and Peter had been married for 23 years, and Gina had been trying to get Peter to go to couples therapy with her for at least five of those years. (Spoiler alert: I met them because she finally succeeded.)

After a few sessions, they talked about those years when Gina was trying to convince Peter to go to couples therapy. What had they each been thinking? What had Gina tried, and why did Peter refuse? What was different this time?

As Gina explained it, when she first brought up the idea and Peter refused, she felt it was because he didn't care enough about her or the relationship to put in the work. Peter didn't say that, exactly, but the reasons he gave left her with that impression. He said she was the one who was having a problem, so she should go to therapy. He said he didn't want some stranger telling them what to do. He said they could work out their own problems.

Gina felt that if Peter really cared about her, he'd be willing to try something she felt might help them. Or at least go along because it might help *her* feel better. Instead, he kept offering lame excuses. They were stuck like that for five years. Even when she threatened divorce—which she didn't want—Peter just resisted. He told her that if she's that unhappy, she could divorce him. But she was the one with the problem. If she'd stop being so dissatisfied, he'd be fine.

Sound familiar?

Women Want to Do Couples Therapy. Men Don't

Here's what I've heard from people who are trying to convince their reluctant partners to try couples therapy. Let me be more specific: Here's what I've heard from women who are trying to convince their reluctant male partners to try couples therapy. I have seen some situations where it's the other way around, but it's rare. Overwhelmingly, it's women who want to do couples therapy and men who resist.

So let's say you're a woman who's been trying, and failing, to convince your male partner to try couples therapy. (If you're a man in this situation—or if you're the resistant partner—read on anyway.)

You've suggested, requested, cajoled, demanded, bribed, threatened. You've carefully timed the conversation to catch him when he might be receptive, and you've blurted it out when you're in the middle of a fight. You've couched it in I statements, you've used active listening, you've applied nonviolent communication.

You've buttered him up, and you've insulted his character. You've cried, pleaded, reasoned, shouted, and punished with silence. You've gone on strike, and you've made extra efforts to be generous.

You've withheld sex, affection, and even basic civility, and you've showered him with attention.

None of it has worked.

You're at the point where all you can think of is to end the relationship. You've already threatened that too, repeatedly. But you really don't want that, if there's a way to be happy about staying together.

How can you get him to see that couples therapy is at least worth a try? Why is he so stubborn, so clueless, so uncaring?

Why Women Think Men Resist Couples Therapy

If you want to get him to change his mind and try couples therapy, you'll need to understand why he's resisting the idea.

I've asked lots of women why they think their guy resisted coming to couples therapy. Here's a top-ten list of their theories:

10) He won't go to therapy because men don't like asking for directions—it threatens their masculinity.

9) He thinks we should be able to solve our own problems.

8) He doesn't want to talk about our personal stuff with a stranger.

7) He thinks therapy is for weak/stupid/crazy people.

6) He thinks therapy is a waste of time and money.

5) He thinks the therapist will side with me and the two of us will gang up on him.

4) He thinks therapists, even male ones, are prejudiced against men.

3) He thinks the therapist will tell us to break up.

2) He tells me the problem is that I'm unhappy, so I should be the one to get therapy.

And the number one reason women think men won't do couples therapy:

1) He doesn't care about me, even when I tell him how much pain I'm in.

All plausible reasons—in fact, many of them are reasons that men themselves often say. No wonder women think those are the reasons. There's just one catch:

Every one of these misses the actual reason completely.

I'll get to that actual reason in a moment. But I want to address that number one reason that a lot of women say they think is why he won't come to therapy: He doesn't care.

If you really believe your guy doesn't care about you, there's no point trying to get him to couples therapy. If you really believe he doesn't care about you, in the sense that he's indifferent to your pain or happiness, leave him.

You haven't left him yet, at least in part, because you know, or at least suspect, that he *does* care about you. He may not show it much, or in ways you want, but the problem isn't lack of caring. He gets angry, or shuts down, not because he doesn't care, but because he does. You're important to him, just like he's important to you or you wouldn't be trying so hard to make things better with him.

So if those aren't the reasons he resists, what is?

Why He's Actually Resisting Couples Therapy

He resists because he's terrified.

And not only is he terrified, but **he's *right* to be terrified.**

Every one of those reasons in the top ten list has a basis in some guys' experience. And every one of those reasons is a proxy for the big one:

He's afraid he'll lose you.

He's worried that couples therapy will lead to breaking up. And that's not a crazy worry. You know people whose relationships have ended after they did couples therapy, and so does he.

And when you give him the ultimatum that says it's either couples therapy or divorce, you're just confirming how precarious the situation is.

So his worry isn't paranoid. It's actually pretty sensible.

Now do you see why all your efforts to get him to come to couples therapy haven't worked? It's not that your reasons for wanting to do it are bad, and it's not that he doesn't care. It's that he's scared, and your very understandable frustration with him just increases his fear.

And, of course, he's a guy—he won't even tell himself that he's scared, let alone you.

So instead of recognizing his fear, he makes up a lot of objections, all of which have some basis in reality, but none of which actually address his fear. Or he gets all reasonable, and acts like you're the one with the emotional problem. Or he gets angry and shouts at you. Or he just shuts down completely.

That's what you're dealing with. **Arguing, cajoling, and threatening don't tend to reduce someone's fear.** They increase it. You know how unreasonable and reactive you get when he denies or minimizes how you feel? That's how he gets too. The trouble is, he doesn't realize that's what he's doing, any more than you do when you're doing it.

So what do you do? Do you have to give up what you want? Of course not. What you want isn't crazy or wrong either. If you could accept the situation as it is, you wouldn't be pushing so hard to do something different.

You don't have to give up on the idea of trying couples therapy. But you do need to approach your partner differently.

And I don't mean finding another way to convince him. You've tried all of those.

Gather Your Thoughts

Write down your impressions as you consider these questions:

1. Have you ever resisted an idea your partner has suggested? If so, why were you resisting? You might have simply disagreed, but you might also have resisted because of how your partner was trying to convince you. Was there some of each of those reasons in your resistance?
2. If you have resisted an idea from your partner, how successful was your partner in convincing you to go along with their idea? If they didn't succeed, why not? If they did, what worked for you?
3. How successful have you been talking someone out of their worry by citing the facts, or criticizing their character, or accusing them of being selfish? How successful have those approaches been when someone tries them with you when you're worried about something?
4. Think of a time when someone helped you feel less worried about something. What did they do or say that helped you relax?

The "Oh, Shit!" Moment

Let's revisit Gina and Peter. Recall that Gina had been trying for years to convince Peter to try couples therapy with her, to no avail. She finally succeeded—they were sitting in my office.

In the first session we talked about stability and intimacy in the context of their relationship. Like so many couples, they began to see how their focus on stability had led them down the death spiral for intimacy. Over the course of a few sessions, as we talked about a lot of the same ideas you've been reading about in this book, they reported that they were bickering less and talking more. They still had difficult moments, but they weren't escalating as they had before. So I asked them why they thought that was happening.

Peter said our sessions seem to be helping. But he added, "I think it started to get better even before our first session." And he gave Gina credit for it. In fact, he said, it was a conversation she initiated that finally convinced him to try couples therapy, after years of rejecting the idea.

"I don't remember exactly what she said. But I could tell right away she wasn't yelling at me or telling me I was inconsiderate. She just wanted to know what worried me about trying couples therapy. That got me thinking about it in a different way—I was always coming up with reasons why it's a bad idea, or unnecessary, but I never thought about why it worried me. And she really listened. She didn't try to deny what I was saying. She even seemed to understand."

Gina nodded. "I don't know how I realized it. Maybe it was desperation, because nothing was working. But one day I was thinking about how unreasonable Peter was, and how uncaring he seemed when I said I was unhappy and wanted to try therapy. And then I thought about the Peter that I knew—he's warm and caring and considerate, or at least he used to be. And I thought, it can't be that he's turned bad. He says he loves me and I believe he does. What's going on? I guess what I realized was that I don't know. I just don't know. But there must be something he's worried about. So I asked him—really asked him, not to talk him out of it, but to find out."

When Gina decided to ask Peter what was worrying him about trying couples therapy, she didn't know how that would go. It might have precipitated a bad fight, as the topic so often had. But she took the risk. And Peter was able to rise to the occasion—also not a foregone conclusion.

Peter said the key thing for him was that she took his worries seriously. "I thought about it, and told her what I think was worrying me is that we'd split up if we did couples therapy. I'd lose her. And she didn't tell me I shouldn't worry. She told me she worries about that too. That really got to me. I knew then we needed to do something."

What Gina and Peter were experiencing in that conversation was what I like to call the **"Oh, shit!" moment**.

It's not the "Oh, shit!" you say when you hit your thumb with a hammer. Instead, it's more like, "Oh, shit—*that's* why we're having this problem." **It's when you realize there are good reasons the other person is disagreeing with you.** It's not an "Aha!" moment, because you still disagree. The problem is still there. But you're not squabbling about it anymore.

And when that happens, you can hear each other, and feel heard.

Notice that Peter didn't remember exactly what Gina said—because that wasn't what made the difference. And how she planned out how to say it wasn't what made the difference either.

What made the difference is what Gina was *actually* thinking and feeling, not what she tried to sound like. What she was actually thinking and feeling was curiosity and compassion, rather than condescension and hostility.

As we talked about that conversation in our session, and Peter was able to think without being defensive, he recognized how much condescension and hostility he had been directing toward Gina for years, and he felt deeply sorry. Gina was also able to see how her anger, however understandable, reinforced Peter's defensiveness.

Gather Your Thoughts

Write down your impressions as you consider these questions:
1. As you think about Gina and Peter's story, how do you judge them? I'm inviting you to consider mixed feelings. Was Gina too willing to let go of her anger over how he had dismissed her

feelings for so long? Why was it up to Gina to approach Peter differently? Why couldn't Peter be expected to initiate the solution? Does it always have to be up to women to accommodate men's stubbornness or cluelessness?

2. If you accept my premise that, overwhelmingly, it's women who want to do couples therapy and men who resist, how would you explain the phenomenon? (Of course, I didn't say it's true for *every* couple. I've met quite a few exceptions—maybe you and your partner are one of them.)
3. If you're in a situation similar to Gina—you're a woman trying to convince your male partner to try couples therapy—what are you thinking now? How might you apply what you take from Gina and Peter's story?
4. If you're in a situation similar to Peter, how might you apply what you take from their story?
5. If you think couples therapy would be a good idea for you and your partner, do you feel able to talk to your partner? If so, when will you do it? How about now?

Part III

Be the Change

Chapter 10

Being the Change: Introduction

Did You Skip Parts I and II?

If you skipped to this part of the book in hopes of learning how to turn things around quickly—which is why you got this book, after all—I sympathize. If I were checking out this book during a crisis in my relationship, that's what I'd do too.

If that works for you, great! But I urge you to go back and do the work of Parts I and II. **Everything from here on assumes you've done the work up to now.**

Now What?

You've learned about **stability** and **intimacy**—why they're both important, why **they require different and sometimes conflicting skills,** and the mindset of **faith** that lets you acquire and implement those skills. You've assessed your relationship in terms of stability and intimacy. In Chapter 4 you considered a variety of common relationship issues, and identified particular areas where you do well and where you don't.

If your partner has also been participating in the work you've been doing, either by doing the exercises independently or at least talking with you about your responses, I hope you're already noticing some positive changes. Just the fact that you're both willing to work on it is a step forward.

Even if you're doing this work by yourself and haven't talked with your partner about it, you've already started to "be the change" that you're looking for.

Now we're going to get specific. In this set of chapters we'll look at the problems you're having and create action plans to deal with them.

How to Use This Part of the Book

Each chapter in this part of the book covers a general topic area that can involve one or more of the relationship issues you considered in Chapter 4. This is only a sampling of potential topics, but I've selected topics that I've heard a lot about from couples I've worked with. Of course, each of these topics could take up a whole book—we're just hitting some representative examples.

For each topic, I'll present some scenarios. I'll ask you questions designed to help you apply what you've learned. When you write your responses, note down the page number of the question so you can easily find which question you're answering.

In addition to asking you questions, I'll offer suggestions to consider. You might notice a change in my tone when I make suggestions, as I step away from therapist mode and offer ideas that reflect my own experiences and preferences. Some of my ideas might challenge your assumptions or values.

You might not like some of my suggestions. Your experiences and preferences undoubtedly differ from mine. **If you don't like one of my suggestions, don't use it—but even the ones you reject will get you thinking.**

At the end of each chapter, you'll be asked to apply its lessons to your own situation by making an action plan. Some of the scenarios are particularly relevant to your own situation, others less so. But even the scenarios illustrating problems you aren't experiencing can help you practice applying the skills you've learned.

Of course, **I won't tell you what to put in your action plan— you know your life, and I don't.** Instead, I'll ask you questions designed to help you figure out for yourself what to do. But it's important that you **write down your action plan** for each topic. If your action plan for a specific topic is simply, "No action needed," write that down.

Some of your action plans might be to simply learn to live with a situation you can't change. If you can actually do that—not merely live with a situation, but live with it without resentment—then you've come up with a solution. Other action plans might call for you to tell your partner how you feel about something you want to change, or to make changes yourself with or without your partner, or even to decide to separate.

Once you've made an action plan, you'll need to act on it. That's where faith, and its cousin courage, come in.

What About Couples Therapy?

Most of the scenarios we'll be looking at involve talking with your partner about potentially hard topics. **Couples therapy is worth considering when you've tried to have a conversation repeatedly and it hasn't gone well.** I don't always mention it in my suggestions, but you might consider it.

One caveat: **Don't use couples therapy as a substitute for bringing up a hard topic.** If you can't even tell your partner what you need to talk about, couples therapy won't help you. If you're afraid of your partner's reaction, couples therapy isn't safe. And if you're not afraid of their reaction, but just want to soften the blow, then waiting to tell them something important until you're in therapy will have the opposite effect: it will leave them feeling blindsided.

Do You Really Want to Risk Change?

When I used to practice clinical hypnosis, I would sometimes work with a client who wanted to stop smoking cigarettes. We'd talk about how they used smoking in their lives and how hypnosis can help. Then I would ask, "When would you like to quit?"

The people who would say, "as soon as I finish this carton" or "next week when I have some time off" or "by my daughter's wedding in the fall" were saying, quite explicitly, they don't want to quit, at least not now. Not surprisingly, they rarely did.

The people who would say, "I really want to quit yesterday" or "I'm ready right now" were, of course, in a better frame of mind to be able to quit. That didn't always mean that cold turkey was the way to go. For many of them, a plan involving tapering off, medication assistance, and social support was how they did it. But they were ready to do what it takes immediately.

You're in that situation. **You're facing painful realities in your relationship, and you want to make it better. When do you want**

to start? It's a legitimate choice to say you're not ready—but don't blame your partner if you make that choice.

The Meta-Serenity Prayer

You might be familiar with the Serenity Prayer, used in 12-step programs such as AA and widely quoted more generally:

God grant me the serenity to accept the things I cannot change, courage to change the things I can, and wisdom to know the difference.

The Serenity Prayer is popular for good reason. It succinctly lays out what we need when we're facing hard choices.

But I want to add another piece to the prayer. I call it the "Meta-Serenity Prayer":

God grant me the serenity to accept that I can't always tell the difference between what I cannot change and what I can. And grant me courage to act anyway.

I've talked about faith as not merely accepting reality, but accepting that it's right to be what it is, even when it's painful and difficult to understand. **The Meta-Serenity Prayer recognizes that, indeed, reality is often difficult to understand.** You're not always going to know what you can change and what you can't.

But we're responsible for making choices anyway, even when we don't know for sure what the right choices are. To do something is a choice, and to do nothing is a choice. The Meta-Serenity Prayer asks for courage to make that choice, even without knowing how it will turn out.

You're doing the work in this book because you want to change things for the better. You're about to consider possibilities, and you won't know for sure exactly what will happen if you act on them. Whether you decide to try something you haven't tried, or leave things as they are, you're making a choice either way. **May you have the faith and courage to choose your path.**

Chapter 11

Parenting

Having/Not Having a Child

Scenario 1:
You have found someone and you're in love. You're both in your twenties or thirties. You've been dating for six months and want to move in together. You're looking for a lifetime partner, and this person feels like "the one."

The two of you haven't talked about whether you want to have children or not. You know how you feel about it, and you're worried that your partner feels the opposite. They haven't said so directly, but they seem to have hinted at how they feel.

1. What would you do in this scenario?
2. Do you know of people who have been in this situation? What do you know about how they handled it? What did you learn from their experience?

3. Have you been in a similar situation in the past? If so, what did you do? How did it turn out?

Scenario 1: Suggestions

I started you off easy—this one is a no-brainer. **You need to talk to your partner explicitly about this.** As in, "We need to talk about whether we want children. I do (or I don't, or I'm ambivalent). What about you?"

You might be relieved by their answer, and you might be distressed by it. But you've got to talk about it. This is either a classic deal-breaker, or a major point of compatibility. You need to know either way.

Scenario 2 (continuation of Scenario 1):

You go ahead and have the conversation. You're sure you want to have a child. Your partner says they don't want to now, and had always assumed they never would, but since you want to they might consider it for the future. You love your partner and don't want to lose the relationship, but you don't want to wait so long for a child that it never happens.

1. If you're the one wanting to have a child, what do you do in this situation? What if your partner says, in effect, it's okay if you have a child, but they don't want to be involved?
2. If you're the one who has never wanted to have a child, what do you do? What if your partner says, in effect, that if they go ahead and have a child they won't expect you to be involved in parenting?

Scenario 2: Suggestions

I've seen this situation quite a few times. Sometimes the partner who doesn't want to have a child warms up to the idea over time, and it turns out fine. A woman who had never wanted children might find that her misgivings had a lot to do with not having the right partner, and when she gets into a stable, loving relationship, finds she wants to have his children. A man who had never wanted children might have a similar experience, often realizing that his worries about becoming a father were more about problems in prior relationships.

But I've also seen situations where one partner "caves," and agrees because they don't want to lose the relationship. Not a great start. Even then I've seen situations where they fall in love with their new baby. The thing is, you can't count on that. Sometimes you end up with deep resentments, where the partner who wanted the child feels emotionally abandoned and the partner who caved feels that they were coerced.

As in Scenario 1, you need to talk about it. Unlike Scenario 1, this isn't black-and-white. Each partner will need to decide if the relationship is still viable. And it falls to the partner wanting a child to determine how long they are willing to wait.

You don't need to carefully plan how you'll bring it up. In fact, your effort to craft how you'll talk about it is what's keeping you stuck. **What you need is a mindset of faith**, which will let you be simultaneously assertive, respectful, and compassionate. You'll be willing to listen, and won't freak out even if your partner does. You'll recognize that you might not solve this in one or two conversations.

What about the idea that just the one who wants the child can do all the parenting? If you're the one who wants a child, don't suggest that unless you want to be a single parent, because you will be.

Having/Not Having a Child: Action Plan

Are you in a situation like this? If so, what are you going to do? If part of your plan is to talk to your partner, when will you do that? **Why not immediately?**

Write down your action plan.

Child-Rearing Approaches

Scenario 3:

You're both in your late thirties, and have young children—say, ages five and three—together. One of you is determined to give the children a healthy diet, which means organic, no added sugar, not ultra-processed, or similar criteria. And one of you (maybe the same one, maybe not) is determined to protect the children from the effects of excessive screen use, which means prohibiting or severely limiting watching videos or playing games on digital devices. And one of you (could be either one) is determined to keep the children safe by monitoring their physical activities closely and using protective equipment to prevent injuries.

The two of you agree generally that you need to keep your children healthy and safe, but you disagree on the details, which leads to conflict. For example, the parent who focuses on the importance of diet might object when the other parent lets the children have a sugary snack. Or the parent who lets them have the snack might object when the other parent insists on enforcing their dietary restrictions when the children are visiting their grandparents.

Sometimes the conflicts get heated, as each of you feels the other is endangering the children, either by being too permissive or by being too restrictive. You've argued about it repeatedly, often in the presence of the children.

1. Have you experienced something like this scenario? What were the areas you've disagreed about?
2. If you've been in a similar situation, how effective have your arguments been in resolving the conflicts? Has either of you convinced the other to change your views?
3. Have you sometimes tried to placate your partner by pretending to agree to something you actually disagree with, rather than being honest about your disagreement? If so, why? Were you afraid of how an honest discussion of your views might go?

4. Have you sometimes insisted on intervening between your partner and the children, rather than talk about it later? If so, why? Were you afraid lasting damage would be done to the children if you didn't intervene?
5. If you could quantify the negative effects on the children, which is causing them more harm: your partner doing what you disapprove of, or the two of you arguing about it?

Scenario 3: Suggestions

The problem here isn't that you have different views of what it means to keep your children healthy and safe in specific instances. That's normal. It's one of the reasons that having two parents is good for children. They figure out early on that you differ from each other about particular issues, and they learn that sometimes there might be more than one point of view to consider. And they learn from how you handle those differences.

If what they see is the two of you extending respect and deference to each other, setting your relationship above having to be right, they learn that differences can lead to better, more nuanced understandings. If what they see is the two of you arguing as if each of you considers the other a menace to the children, they learn that differences are dangerous.

Remember when I said you might not like some of my suggestions? Here's one that lots of you won't like.

Often in this situation, one of you is the fanatic, and the other is trying to deal with the fanatic. You probably know who you are.

If you're the fanatic, knock it off. Your fanaticism is way worse for your children than whatever benighted ideas your partner has. Whatever your views about diet, screen time, general safety, or insert your favorite child-rearing theory here, you don't have a monopoly on truth, no matter how many internet articles you've read. If your partner resists what you are advocating, it could be because they don't know as much about it as you do, or because they just disagree. But it could also be that they mostly agree and even recognize your relative expertise, but are resisting because you're being self-righteous, and they sense your disrespect.

This tendency is particularly acute when your strong views about what's right leads you to intervene when your partner is handling something with the children in a way you think is wrong. Your partner then angrily accuses you of undermining their parenting, because that's what you're doing.

Of course, **if you think it's only your partner who is the fanatic, and you're just being reasonable, look again.** You don't have a monopoly on truth either. You know those moments you get so angry about, when your partner intervenes? Your anger is a big factor in why they do that. They're protecting the children from you. If you weren't so offended and could actually talk about your disagreements respectfully, you might have a chance at being heard.

Ironically, if you're about to intervene between your partner and the kids, and realize that **the situation isn't actually dangerous**, you'll relax and let it play out. If you're the other partner, and you realize that **you don't have to be insulted** by your partner's well-intentioned effort to help, you'll relax and not get angry about it. If you're not panicked, and have some forbearance for your partner's occasional lack of grace, these situations will be far less fraught.

I often recite Philip Larkin's poem "This Be the Verse" to couples I'm working with when we're talking about parenting differences. (Google it.) The main idea of the poem, hilariously expressed, is that no matter what you do, you're going to be messing up your kids (he uses a more graphic word). I like to observe that **parenting style is important, but as long as you're well this side of truly horrible it's not nearly as important as we worry that it is.** Kids turn out fine, or don't, across the spectrum of parenting practices. There are a lot of factors besides parenting that are at least as determinative of how kids turn out, many of which we have no control over.

If you don't try so hard to get parenting exactly right, you'll find you won't argue about how to do it nearly as much. And when you do disagree, you won't be in panic mode, because the stakes will be lower. Imagine what that will do for your children.

But what if your partner's child-rearing opinions are so opposed to yours that you feel you can't stay with them? What if you consider your partner's ways of parenting to be abusive?

I've met parents who are trying to protect their children from the other parent who really is abusive. I know it happens. If that's what you're dealing with, you need to get yourself and your children safe. If that involves fighting for custody, you need to do what's necessary.

But I've also met parents who define abuse so broadly that there's no room for differences in style or just being somewhat impatient at times. If that's you, that's just another form of fanaticism. It won't serve you, or the children. And, of course, if you are able to rethink your views, you might find that differences you thought intolerable aren't that bad, and you won't need to split up.

Child-Rearing Approaches: Action Plan

Are you in a situation like this? If so, what are you going to do?

Here are some options to consider.

If you recognize yourself as the (relatively) fanatic partner about some issues, can you question your assumptions, back away from your ideologies, and make room for other ideas? If so, will you let your partner know you've been rethinking some of your beliefs? Is an apology in order to address ways you've shown condescension or contempt for their views?

If you recognize yourself as the (relatively) less fanatic partner, can you examine how you've reacted? Can you be honest about how you disagree, while still respecting your partner's views? Is an apology in order to address ways you've shown condescension or contempt for their views?

Whichever role you're in, what you do will be driven by a choice: **Do you want to be right, or in a relationship?**

What's your next step? Write down your action plan.

Chapter 12

Stepparenting

Stepparenting Issues

Scenario 4:
You're both in your mid-forties. It's a second marriage for both of you. One of you has two teenage sons from the first marriage, and the other has no kids. You've known each other for three years, and married and moved in together to a new house a year ago. The kids live with the two of you about half the time.

The older son, age 15, has been the more difficult one since the separation, which happened very shortly before the two of you got together. He has said he considers both of you—especially his parent—responsible for ruining his life.

If you're the stepparent, you have been getting increasingly frustrated with the parent, feeling that they let the older son get away with disrespectful behavior without imposing consequences.

If you're the parent, you often feel caught between your child and your spouse, trying to placate both of them. The tension between the two of you is threatening your marriage.

1. Are you in a similar situation? You could be the parent, the stepparent, or both.
2. If you're the parent, how much does guilt about splitting from your child's parent affect your parenting? How much does anger toward the other parent affect your parenting? This may be hard to quantify, but think about occasions when your emotions about your ex might have made your parenting decisions less effective.
3. If you're the parent, how do you understand the frustration your partner, the stepparent, expresses? Does the stepparent ever have some ideas worth considering, even though you have way more experience parenting your child?
4. If you're the stepparent, how do you understand the parent's sense of being caught between you and your stepchild? If you're familiar with the concept of "mansplaining," regardless of your gender, can you see how the parent might feel about your offering your ideas about how they should parent their child?
5. How have the two of you managed expectations of each other regarding parenting? If relevant, have you discussed expectations about babysitting, school pickups, or relationships with the other bio parent? Have you discussed expectations regarding rules enforcement for the kids?

Scenario 4: Suggestions

Lest I overgeneralize, let me note that I have met people for whom their stepparent was every bit as primary in their lives as their bio parent. Those are the people who tell me, for example, that their stepfather is "Dad," and their bio father was in and out of their lives.

That said, the norm for most families is that stepparenting isn't the same as parenting.

Here's my favorite way of characterizing the difference. A parent can, and often will, impose something contrary to a kid's wishes. The kid might well get angry about whatever the parent is imposing on them. But if a stepparent imposes something on them, the kid won't only get angry about what they're imposing; the kid will get angry that the stepparent is presuming to impose anything at all.

In other words, if you're the kid, you see your parent as a legitimate authority. You might not like their decisions, and you might defy them, but you don't question that they have the right to make them.

But you don't grant that same standing to your stepparent. Hence the "You're not my mother/father" attitude.

What does this mean in practice?

I met a couple a few years ago who were in a similar situation to our scenario. The couple had been to a couples therapist who advised the stepfather that the mother should handle all discipline. Since the stepfather often objected to things his stepson was or wasn't doing, he interpreted this advice as meaning that he should pretty much avoid contact with his stepson, especially if the mother wasn't around. Not surprisingly, this didn't help their relationship.

Fortunately, I can give you the one bit of advice you can count on:

There isn't a single rule that always works.

The idea that the parent is the source of authority, rather than the stepparent, is a good idea. But like so many good ideas, it doesn't tell you what to do in every situation.

Remember when I pointed out in Chapter 6 that **the most important skill you'll ever learn is to be able to accept contradictory truths simultaneously**? This is a great example. Yes, most kids will accept (grudgingly or not) their parent's authority, and will question their stepparent's authority. Yes, that means it usually works better when rules and enforcement come from the parent, not the stepparent. And yes, there are times when the stepparent needs to step into the authority role anyway. And you can't always tell when those times are.

I asked you if the two of you have discussed expectations, because I think it's vital that you talk about them. Whatever agreements you come up with, there's an even more critical expectation: **You should expect that your agreements won't always work in practice.** Stuff will happen you haven't anticipated.

Recall what I said about Philip Larkin's poem. Your parenting is important, but you'll never get it exactly "right." That applies to stepparenting as well. When you realize that, the stakes are lower, and the inevitable disagreements don't turn into death matches.

Stepparenting Issues: Action Plan

Are you in a situation like this? If so, what are you going to do?

Your most basic choices are stark: You can find a way to talk to each other about these issues with mutual respect, openness to questioning your own certainties, and willingness to put your relationship above your parenting ideologies. Or you can keep arguing, stay miserable, and eventually split up. Or you could just go ahead and decide to split up, if you're convinced there's no other solution.

If you're the stepparent, how well do you understand your partner's frustrations, especially if they seem caught between you and their child? If you're the parent, how well do you understand your partner's frustrations, especially if they seem to feel disempowered in their own home?

Have the two of you had conversations in a spirit of curiosity, each of you trying to understand the other's point of view? Have you talked about expectations of each other, recognizing that there will always be some gray areas?

What's your next step? Write down your action plan.

Chapter 13

Marriage

Should You Get Married or Not?

Scenario 5:
You've been together for several years, living together for most of that time. One of you—let's say the woman in a hetero couple—would prefer to get married, and the other—the man—wants to keep the arrangement as it is, living together and monogamous but not married. You talked about it early on just enough to know each other's preference, but it hasn't been a serious issue until recently. (Yes, it's not always the woman who wants to get married and the man who resists, but that's much more common than the other way around.)

If you're the woman, you've become increasingly dissatisfied with not being married. If you're the man, you've noticed her dissatisfaction. When you've talked with each other about it, the conversations have become arguments. You're both beginning to have doubts about whether your relationship can continue.

1. Are you in a similar situation? Or were you ever in a similar situation, with either a current partner or one in the past?
2. Whichever side of the issue you're on, do you understand your partner's position? If you're the one who wants to get married, do you understand your partner's misgivings? If you're the one who doesn't want to get married, do you understand why your partner does?
3. Are you concerned that this is a deal-breaker?

Scenario 5: Suggestions

Start by questioning your own assumptions. (That's always a good place to start.)

If you're the one who wants to get married, why? Allow me to demolish some common answers to that question, answers that will get you nowhere with your partner. But don't worry—I'll suggest a better answer.

If you think getting married will guarantee or even strengthen your commitment to each other over the long haul, think again. Marriage doesn't guarantee anything. Your partner can probably cite examples of couples you both know who were fine until they got married, after which things went to hell. That's not just coincidence. Marriage changes the emotional landscape, often in ways people aren't prepared for.

If you think your partner's reluctance to marry you means they don't really love you, think again. Many people resist marriage not because they don't love their partner, but because they do—and they don't want to risk destroying a relationship by changing it. Your partner may be wondering why your love for them is so conditional that you are willing to risk it just to be able to say you're married.

Of course, if you do seriously doubt your partner's commitment to you, or their love for you, that's a reason to doubt whether the relationship is viable. But that's not about marriage per se. Just because they don't want to get married doesn't mean they don't love you or aren't committed to your relationship.

Then why get married?

Get married if you want to dedicate your relationship to something beyond just the two of you. When you get married, you're no longer just yourself, and the two of you are no longer just the two of you. Instead, you've become part of something you don't get to define. Your families, your friends, your workmates, your broader communities, and your governments are all involved in your marriage. In religious terms, you're not just celebrating your love for each other; you're getting married before God. It's not just about you anymore.

In a traditional Jewish wedding, the couple stands under a *chuppah*—a canopy with open sides. The open sides symbolize, to put it more bluntly than usually stated, that when you're in bed with each other the whole community is in there with you. That's what you're getting when you get married. Everybody's got a piece of you. There's protection in that system for you, especially if you're in a vulnerable position (as women have traditionally been), and there's also intrusion in that system for you.

Get married if you *like* that idea.

Lest I sound cynical, let me note that I *do* like that idea. **There's a kind of growth that can happen in a marriage that I don't think is available any other way.** To recognize that your relationship matters not just to the two of you, but to the wider world, changes how you experience the inevitable annoyances that come with being human.

Let's look at the other side. If you're the one who doesn't want to get married, why don't you? In a spirit of fairness, let me demolish some of your answers too, and offer a good one.

If you're worried that marriage might mess up a good thing, you're right—that could happen. But **if your reluctance is**

distressing enough to your partner, you don't have the good thing you think you have. You won't talk her out of wanting it, simply because her wanting it is just as valid as your not wanting it.

If you don't like the idea of other people, especially the government, having a say in your relationship, you're entitled to your opinion, but it won't convince your partner. Divorce laws exist primarily to protect vulnerable spouses and children in case a couple splits up. You can avoid divorce by avoiding marriage, but you're also depriving your partner of that protection. **Even if you don't agree that divorce offers protection, you won't talk your partner out of wanting marriage if she thinks it does.** She'll just see you as not caring enough about her to give her that protection.

And her wanting marriage isn't just about legal protection. It's about how you're viewed by your families, friends, and everyone else. **Your reluctance is depriving her of the sense of acceptance that comes with being married.** If you try to deny that marriage offers that sense of acceptance, especially for women, you'll get nowhere. She'll see you as yet another arrogant man denying women's experience—because that's what you'd be.

Rather than deny her reality, you could argue that you think it should be resisted. In other words, you could say that you recognize that others would view you differently, generally in positive ways, if you were married. But you could assert that you object to that system, and feel that the two of you should be able to define your own relationship without being bound by social convention.

And that, I think, is your best argument. Not because it will convince her—it won't—but because it at least acknowledges her experience. You're saying, in effect, that you don't want marriage precisely because you *don't* like the idea of others having a stake in your relationship. I noted earlier that I *do*, but I can see the other side. You might feel that the emotional and spiritual benefits some of us see in marriage aren't worth the loss of autonomy. **It's not an** argument about facts. It's about what you value, and how you balance conflicting priorities.

Of course, she might hear your principled stand as condescending, clueless of women's experience, unempathetic, or some combination of those—and maybe she has a point. But at least you're not denying reality, even if you want to resist it.

When you stop trying to convince each other that your priorities are wrong, you at least have a shot at honest conversations that don't turn into shouting matches. The danger you both face is that this could be a deal-breaker.

Scenario 6:
As in Scenario 5, you've been together for several years, but in this scenario, you've talked about marriage before and both said you want it to happen.

If you're the woman, you've been repeatedly disappointed as obvious opportunities (birthdays, Valentines Day, romantic dates) have come and gone without a proposal. If you're the man, you're feeling increasingly pressured. The two of you have argued about it, and the more you argue, the more you're at an impasse. She: If he would just propose, we'd stop arguing so much. He: If we stopped arguing so much, I'd want to propose.

1. Are you in a similar situation? Or if you're married, were you in a similar situation before you got married?
2. If you're the one who is waiting for a proposal, why is it important to you that your partner be the one to propose? Do you understand why they haven't proposed yet? Have you asked in a spirit of curiosity, rather than anger?
3. If you're the one who hasn't proposed, what's stopping you? Do you understand how your partner feels about it? Have you asked in a spirit of curiosity, rather than anger?

Scenario 6: Suggestions

I've seen this situation many times. If you're the man in this scenario, you're not objecting to marriage per se, and you love your partner. But the more you sense your partner's disappointment and anger, the more it feels like you're in a double-bind. If you just propose so she'll stop harassing you about it, you'll feel coerced—the very opposite of how you want to feel in a marriage. And if you wait until you can propose purely of your own volition, without feeling pressured, you'll be waiting forever, because just the fact of her wanting it so much constitutes pressure.

If you're the woman in this situation, you might even recognize the double-bind he's in. But you can't pretend that you're fine with the status quo. Your impatience is just as valid as his resistance.

The longer this goes on, the more you each doubt whether you can stay together. Why would you want to get married when you've been fighting so much and making each other miserable?

The way out of this impasse is simple, but not easy. And whether you can pull it off depends on how much good will is left in the emotional bank account.

What's the simple way out? **It's to recognize the sheer absurdity of the situation.** When you can laugh about it, you have a chance to back off from your absolute stances and figure out what to do.

For the woman, this might mean giving up on her expectation of a surprise proposal. For the man, this definitely means giving up on an expectation of no pressure. Many couples I've worked with on this issue end up just agreeing on a rough time frame for when they're going to get married, and then the man finds a fun way to propose. The proposal itself is no surprise, but maybe the timing is. Or maybe they just don't worry about a proposal, and get on with planning their wedding. Or maybe the one who's been waiting—usually the woman—just goes ahead and proposes to her partner. When you've relaxed and appreciated the absurdity of the impasse, any of those is a fine solution.

Recognizing the absurdity is simple, but not easy, because you've probably said a lot of hurtful things to each other in those arguments you've been having. If your relationship is resilient—in other words, if you have a healthy balance in the emotional bank account—you can see the hurt feelings as just a few blips, those rare times when you get angry with each other and then get over it.

But if you're overdrawn in the emotional bank account, this is hard to get past. You might even recognize the absurdity of the impasse, but you'd have a hard time laughing about it. This could become a deal-breaker if you're not able to replenish the emotional bank account.

Should You Get Married or Not? Action Plan

Are you in a similar situation? If so, what are you going to do?

As usual in these scenarios, if you want to solve this you'll need to have honest, respectful conversations. You could keep waiting, but you know that hasn't been working. This calls for action.

What's your next step? Write down your action plan.

Chapter 14

Finances

Financial Differences

Scenario 7:
You're both in your mid-forties, married for fifteen years, with two kids in school. You're both employed outside the home. One of you gets paid about three times more than the other . When you first got together, your incomes were similar, and then the one of you who now gets paid more took a cut in income for a few years to get an advanced professional credential, while the other supported the family financially.

Both partners have demanding work schedules, but one of you is nearly always the one who juggles work responsibilities to cover doctor's appointments, school meetings, lessons, practices, and other kids' needs. Lately this has led to arguments between the two of you, with each of you feeling your contributions to the family are taken for granted, while your burden is unacknowledged.

Another area of contention is how you each spend money. You have different hobbies, different tolerance for financial risk, and different priorities. It seems like almost anything—a package delivery, a trip to the grocery store, a night out—can lead to an argument.

1. Are you in a similar situation? Do you know other couples in this situation? Did you grow up with parents in some version of this situation?
2. If you're in a hetero couple, how does gender play into this? For example, if you're the woman, do you find you're taking on more of the child-related tasks and appointments even if you're the one who gets paid more? If you're the man and get paid less, do you feel somehow less valid as a provider?
3. Whichever role you're in, have you been able to talk about these issues productively?
4. If, as in the scenario, one of you stayed employed to allow the other to get training to advance their career, has that come up in arguments?
5. How much do you each know about your finances? Do you each know how much the other is paid? Do you both know about all financial accounts, including savings, checking, loans, and credit cards?
6. Which one of you manages money—paying bills, moving money to cover checks, and so on?
7. Do you have a budget that you try to adhere to? If so, how did you arrive at it?
8. How do you decide when you need to check with each other before making a purchase?

Scenario 7: Suggestions

How you handle finances depends on how you see yourselves as a couple.

On one end of the spectrum are couples who consider themselves a single economic unit. There's no "yours" and "mine"—it's all "ours." Those couples might argue about particular expenditures or priorities. They might even differ about overall strategies. But even if they maintain some separate accounts, they see their assets and liabilities as shared.

On the other end of the spectrum are couples who keep their finances completely separate. They divide up expenses, often with the understanding that "I pay for these things and you pay for those things." They handle joint expenses by agreeing how much each partner should contribute toward them. They often keep track of how much one partner owes to the other.

Which way is better? I've seen couples who do fine with finances either way, and couples who get into nasty power struggles either way. In that regard, finances is like parenting: You can do okay regardless of your general method, as long as it's not completely horrible.

So I'm not going to endorse either general approach. But I will share some cautionary takes.

If you think you pay for the mortgage and your partner pays for the car insurance, that might not actually be true in a legal sense, at least if you're married (and in some places, even if you're not). Yes, maybe the mortgage comes out of your account and the car insurance comes out of your partner's account. But if you've been together long enough, you could discover that you've both been paying for everything, whether you knew it or not.

When would you discover this? If you split up and tried to figure out how to divide things up. Depending on where you live, all your assets might get lumped together retroactive to when you got together. It wouldn't matter which account was used for what, or whose name is or isn't on the account. It's all one big pot.

Those assets could include your earning power. If, as in our scenario, one of you was able to get qualified to earn more due to the other's support as you got your training, the law might consider that earnings bump to be jointly held. Which is to say, even your respective salaries are joint assets.

Aside from legal considerations, you're dealing with some heavy emotions when you struggle about money. Those arguments you're having aren't about what will happen legally if you divorce (unless, of course, that's what you're doing). **Those arguments are about feeling both secure and loved—our old friends, stability and intimacy.**

I asked you above if gender seems to play a role in how you feel about finances, because it often does, based on what I've heard from couples. Many women have told me they resent having to keep a demanding job outside the home when they would rather be raising the kids full-time. This is especially acute when her job pays a lot more than her partner's job, and the decision about how to do child-care is driven by that. Many men have told me that they feel that resentment and find it outrageously unfair, especially when they were the ones who sacrificed to allow their partners to advance professionally.

Then there's the common phenomenon of women assuming a disproportionate share of child-related duties, even when they're the ones with the more demanding outside job. When I hear about that from couples, both the women and the men are frustrated. The women are frustrated because whenever they try to tell their partner how overburdened they are, he gets defensive and cites all the things he does, rather than listening to her and trying to help her feel better. The men are frustrated because it seems like whatever he does is never enough.

Whatever the particulars of the struggles you're going through, you need a way of addressing them that supports both stability and intimacy. Here are some suggestions based on my preferences (your mileage may vary).

For stability, you each need to feel that your basic safety doesn't depend on your partner's mood. This means that you both need access to enough assets to be okay, at least initially, if you suddenly split up in anger. If only one of you controls the money, the other is at greater risk. No matter how much you reassure your partner that you wouldn't leave them destitute even if you split up, neither you nor your partner know for sure how you'd react if, for example, your partner cheated on you. And if you're worried that your partner might cheat on you if they felt financially secure, you have bigger problems than just financial differences. If keeping your partner financially insecure is your solution, you won't have a partner, you'll have an indentured servant. Presumably, that's not what you want. (Or if it is, just split up now.)

You don't have to have everything in joint accounts, though a lot of couples do it that way. Keeping everything in joint accounts requires that both partners are willing to trust that the other wouldn't drain the accounts, either out of anger or out of irresponsibility (say, due to a gambling or spending addiction). For that reason, many couples also maintain separate accounts that their partner couldn't access. The main thing is that each partner would have access to enough funds so that they'd have some safety net if the relationship went sour.

Of course, if you're living on a very tight budget with little or no reserve, this might be impossible. Even then, you can be fine with each other as long as you feel that you're in it together—and that's where intimacy comes in.

For intimacy, you each need to feel that you can be who you are, and can respect who your partner is, even when you differ. You're looking for generosity from each other, not resentment. That's challenging when you're feeling stressed out.

Intimacy also requires that you both have access to the complete financial picture. Even when one of you is the main money manager, you both need to know about all of your assets and debts. And if you try to hide financial information—say, a debt you're trying to pay off before your partner knows about it—you're headed for trouble. Your partner will feel betrayed when they find out about it. And **they probably will find out about it.**

Financial struggles are often a proxy for worries about whether your partner has your back. Are you really on the same team, or is it a competition? If you want your relationship to thrive, you'll need to prioritize being a team.

Financial Differences: Action Plan

Are you having financial issues with your partner? If so, what are you going to do?

Do you trust that your partner wouldn't drain your accounts and leave you destitute, no matter how angry they were? Do you trust that you wouldn't do that to your partner, no matter how angry you were? If you have serious doubts about those questions, can you talk to your partner about them? If you don't feel able to talk to them, what's stopping you? Could you risk it?

Even if you basically trust each other's good will, do you need to discuss restructuring your finances to help both of you feel more secure? Do you need to make sure you both know the full picture of your finances? Do you need to talk about a budget?

What's your next step? Write down your action plan.

Chapter 15

Sex

Problems Having Sex

Scenario 8:
You're both in your late twenties, together for five years, no kids. When you first got together you had an active sex life, but shortly after you moved in together three years ago one of you started to have panic attacks whenever the two of you initiated sex. At first you both thought it was just stress, but then the partner having the attacks realized that they were reactions to sexual abuse that had happened years before—it's PTSD. After the third panic attack, you stopped trying to have sex at all.

The sex-averse partner has been doing talk therapy for over two years, but the fear of another panic attack is still too powerful to consider trying sex again. The sex-desiring partner tries to be understanding, but the prospect of a sexless relationship feels dismal.

The two of you love each other and want to stay together, but this is causing doubts for both of you.

1. Are you in a similar situation? Which role are you in?
2. If you're the sex-averse partner, are you doing therapy specifically designed to address PTSD? Are you sure the panic attacks were triggered by past trauma, or might you have other reasons?
3. If you're the sex-desiring partner, how well do you understand your partner's experience? Have you experienced panic attacks yourself?
4. Have you talked about the situation with each other?

Scenario 8: Suggestions

My suggestion for this scenario is simple: **This calls for couples therapy.** The sex-averse partner is feeling pressured, the sex-desiring partner is feeling frustrated, and you're both feeling powerless. If you've found that talking about it with each other just adds to the pressure and frustration, couples therapy is a good option.

Couples therapy can help get you out of that self-reinforcing misery, assuming you're working with a therapist who is comfortable talking about sex. (You might be amazed how many therapists aren't.)

The reason I asked if you're sure it's a PTSD reaction is that I've seen situations in which a well-meaning trauma-oriented therapist focuses so narrowly on potential trauma effects that they ignore other possibilities. Aversion to sex often results from a negative spiral: something goes wrong in a sexual encounter, either or both parties start to worry that it will happen again, and over time even the prospect of initiating sex triggers severe anxiety. What goes wrong in the first place could be a medical issue, a relational issue, or just a random anxiety attack. It could also be a symptom of a fundamental incompatibility (see Scenario 10 below). Couples therapy can help sort out the possibilities and find a way forward.

Desire Discrepancy

Scenario 9:
You've been together for twenty-five years, and the kids have grown up and left home. You finally have time to focus on yourselves and each other.

Over the years you've had a comfortable sex life. One of you would want to have sex more frequently than the other, but with the distractions and stresses of raising kids the differences in your libidos wasn't much of an issue.

Now that the kids have left, and you have more opportunities to have sex if you both want to, the higher-libido partner has been pressing for more. The lower-libido partner finds this pressure a turnoff, especially when it seems like it should be obvious that they're not in the mood. The higher-libido partner recognizes this and tries to do things to help lighten the load in hopes that their partner will get in the mood, but the frustration of being rejected has led them to stop trying. You can't talk about it without getting into an argument.

1. Are you in a similar situation? If so, which role are you? This kind of discrepancy can happen at any age—it's not just an empty-nester phenomenon.
2. Even if a difference in libidos isn't a problem in your relationship, have you noticed that one of you is more likely to want to initiate sex? If so, how have you handled the difference?

Scenario 9: Suggestions
You might have noticed that I made no assumptions in this scenario about which gender had the higher libido. It's not always the man. I've worked with lots of hetero couples where the woman is the one who wants more frequent sex. There are indeed characteristic differences between men and women in how they relate to sex: usually, women want to feel intimate before they want to get sexual, and men want to get sexual as a way to feel intimate. But that doesn't always mean that men want to get sexual more often.

The problem this couple is having isn't that they have different preferences for how often to have sex. That's nearly universal between any two people—their libidos are unlikely to be perfectly synchronized. No, **their problem is that they can't talk about it.** One feels pressured and misunderstood, and the other feels rejected and misunderstood. When they try to talk about it, they end up fighting for validation, rather than hearing each other.

How can you break this cycle? Here are some suggestions.

First, **check for medical issues**—hormones, medication effects, aftereffects of surgery, etc. Medical issues can directly suppress libido, but they can also trigger a cycle not unlike what we talked about in Scenario 8: something goes wrong, sex becomes associated with anxiety, and frustration ensues.

Then, **check your assumptions.** Do you assume that your partner's lack of interest in sex means that they don't love you? Do you assume that your partner's frustration at your lack of interest in sex means that all they care about is sex, not about you? Do you assume that sex has to be spontaneous, or it's somehow inauthentic? All of these assumptions are death traps for your relationship, and all of them are wrong.

People just vary, for all kinds of complex reasons, in how often they want to have sex. That means that **every couple will occasionally experience moments where one wants to initiate sex and the other isn't in the mood.** How a couple handles that moment is both an indicator of how their intimate life is more generally, and a powerful causal factor in how things will go from there. **Couples that can handle that moment with grace will be fine.** Couples that end up in anger or deep freeze when that moment happens are in deep trouble.

What's handling it with grace? For the person saying no, it means appreciating rather than resenting their partner's desire, and letting them down with compassion. For the person receiving the no, it means appreciating their partner's willingness to be honest rather than placating them by "phoning it in," and responding with kindness.

When you realize that **some discrepancy in libido is the rule, not the exception**, you won't have to see deep relational significance every time one of you proposes sex and the other isn't in the mood. And when you're not panicked about it, some possibilities open up for each of you.

Often the lower-libido person says that they enjoy sex when it happens, but they just don't think about it other times. In other words, they experience responsive libido, but not spontaneous libido. This is particularly common among women. Many of those women have told me that they know sex is good for their relationship, but they aren't likely to initiate it spontaneously—they're just not thinking about it. Their solution is simple: they schedule sex. They set aside time on the calendar when they're going to let themselves get into the mood. Of course, it helps if their partner learns some skills to help them get into the mood.

To see scheduling sex as a solution requires that both partners accept their differences with appreciation and good humor. The lower-libido partner accepts that sex is important to the higher-desire partner as an expression of love. The higher-libido partner accepts that their partner's responsive libido is an authentic expression of desire. And they handle moments when they're out of sync with generosity and compassion.

Differences in Erotic Orientation

Scenario 10:
You've been a couple for five years, during which you've had a sex life both of you would describe as "meh." Finally, a few weeks ago, one of you told the other that they figured out that they're a sexual submissive—that is, their fantasies are of being dominated,

restrained, and taken with force. The vanilla sex the two of you have been having just doesn't do it for them.

You love each other, but this has precipitated a crisis, because the other partner is completely turned off by the prospect of trying to dominate someone sexually.

1. Are you in a similar situation? It doesn't have to involve dominance/submission. It could be anything that one partner strongly wants, and the other strongly doesn't want.
2. Do you have some sexual fantasies that you're afraid to tell your partner about? Do you let yourself know your sexual fantasies?
3. Do you worry your partner has some fantasies that you would be appalled by?

Scenario 10: Suggestions

Erotic orientation refers to the stuff that turns you on. It's not the same as sexual orientation, a term which is usually used narrowly to mean which gender(s) you might want to have sex with. Lots of people who identify as heterosexual (sexual orientation) have homoerotic fantasies (erotic orientation)—in some research, over half of women and close to a third of men.

Erotic orientation varies widely. It's amazing what turns some people on. Google "types of kinks" and appreciate (or be appalled by) the variety.

No two people have exactly the same repertoire of fantasies or activities that they find sexually arousing. And your own repertoire can expand and change. Part of what keeps a couple's sex life exciting is when they explore new possibilities, especially in the domain of fantasy.

The problem some couples, like the one in our scenario, encounter is when their respective erotic orientations aren't merely different, but incompatible.

Early in my practice I met a couple from whom I learned a lot about this problem. The woman, an attorney known for her aggressive take-no-prisoners style, had discovered years before that she's a sexual submissive, and needed not only domination from her partner but humiliation. (This is similar to the phenomenon of a male CEO going to a dominatrix.) Her husband, a big, gruff construction worker, couldn't do it. He could *pretend* to want to humiliate her, but his heart wasn't in it—he was only doing it to please her. What she wanted was someone who actually got off on being a bully.

Their solution was to find someone through a listserv online (this was in the early days of the internet) who would order her to do various gruesome things to herself, some of which landed her in the emergency room. This had worked for them for several years, but the man was having trouble tolerating it. Our work didn't solve that problem completely, but after a few sessions they both reported being able to talk about it with each other much more easily than before.

If you're worried your erotic orientations aren't just different but might be incompatible, you're in one of those situations I classify as a growing pain, not a deal-breaker. In other words, don't break up too soon. Sometimes a couple can explore their fantasies with each other and discover that they can broaden their repertoire in ways that satisfy both of them. And even if you eventually decide that it won't work to stay together, what you'll learn in that exploration will help you in any future relationship.

Sexual Issues: Action Plan

If you've having sexual issues in your relationship, you're going to need to talk about them. What can you do to start the conversation? If you think couples therapy would facilitate that conversation, will you propose it to your partner?

Have you found it difficult to talk about sex at all? How will you start to practice that skill?

Are you able to tell your partner what you like or don't like when things are happening? Can you accept your partner's guidance without resentment?

What's your next step? Write down your action plan.

Chapter 16

Betrayal

Infidelity

Scenario 11:
You've been together for fifteen years with a mutual promise of monogamy, and one of you has just confessed to the other about a sexual affair with a co-worker.

1. Are you currently or have you ever been in a similar situation? Were you the one who cheated, or the one who was cheated on?
2. If you've experienced infidelity (from either side) in the past, how well have you healed from it? Are you still together as a couple, or did you split up?
3. If you're the one who was cheated on, have you been able to forgive your partner? What would forgiveness mean to you? Can you let go of most of the anger, even if you're not sure you can rebuild trust?

4. If you're the one who cheated, do you have a clear sense of how it happened? Did you know it was wrong, or were you feeling that if your partner didn't find out it wasn't wrong? If you did know it was wrong, do you know what you were telling yourself to allow yourself to violate your own values? Have you been able to forgive yourself, so you can work on learning what you need to learn?

Scenario 11: Suggestions

As I mentioned in Chapter 7, I've written a book on this topic, called *Betrayal and Forgiveness: How to Navigate the Turmoil and Learn to Trust Again*. So my main suggestion if you're in this situation is to read that book—it's available wherever you got this one.

You'll learn why **forgiveness is separate from trust**—in other words, you can forgive someone you don't trust and don't intend to restore a relationship with. You'll learn why forgiveness is important for both the betrayer and the betrayed, when you shouldn't forgive, and three steps to help you forgive when you're ready. And you'll learn how to rebuild trust if you choose to, or how to move on if you need to.

If you've just found out about your partner's infidelity, or just confessed to it yourself, you're some combination of angry, incredulous, confused, ashamed, and terrified. **You just need to know that it will get better—because it will.**

As I mentioned in Chapter 5, **infidelity is not necessarily a deal-breaker.** I've worked with many couples for whom the crisis leads to growth, and many of them stay together and are grateful for what they've learned through the crisis. They look back on the infidelity as a painful set of lessons from which they benefited. Even couples who eventually decide to split up can benefit from the growth that comes from working through the crisis.

The thing to avoid is splitting up in a panic. That's especially true if you have children together.

Lying

Scenario 12:

You've been married for five years. One of you noticed the smell of tobacco on the other and asked if they had been smoking. The other denied it, and said the smell came from a friend who was smoking. After a tense conversation, they then admitted that they had bummed a cigarette from the friend, but insisted that this was the first time they had smoked since quitting three years ago.

1. Have you experienced something like this? Which role were you in?
2. If you're the partner who was lied to, why do you think your partner lied to you? Have you ever lied to your partner? How difficult has it been for you to forgive your partner for lying to you?
3. If you're the partner who lied, do you know why? It might be as simple as not wanting to incur your partner's anger, but might there be other reasons?

Scenario 13:

You're been married for five years. One of you just found out that the other was fired—two months ago. Every workday during those two months, the spouse who was fired got dressed and left the house as if for work, and would make up anecdotes about their workday if they were asked about it when they got home. They were only caught when the other spouse went for a medical appointment and was told their insurance was no longer in effect.

1. Have you experienced something like this? Which role were you in?
2. If you're the partner who was lied to, why do you think your partner lied to you? Have you ever lied to your partner? How difficult has it been for you to forgive your partner for lying to you?

3. If you're the partner who lied, do you know why? It might be as simple as not wanting to incur your partner's anger, but might there be other reasons?

Scenarios 12 and 13: Suggestions

Everyone lies. I don't mean to justify bad behavior, but if you think you've never lied, especially to your partner, you're lying to yourself. At the least, you've lied about how you feel about something, or lied by disguising or sugarcoating a detail, or lied by omission. You've decided not to tell them something because it might upset them, or you've been selective about which details to include, or you've reassured them about something without any idea how it will turn out. You've exaggerated for effect. You've lied and not even realized you're lying.

Jonathan Haidt writes about this in his book *The Righteous Mind*. When I read his description of how he realized he had lied to his wife without even knowing it until he thought about it later, a similar story occurred to me. I was asked at my granddaughter's naming to say something about my grandmother, after whom she was named. So I told a story I remembered about how my grandmother had stared down a vicious dog that had chased me on our block when I was a child. It wasn't until later that I realized I had embellished the story—the dog had already left before my grandmother walked me home. The story was a lot more evocative of my grandmother's toughness the way I told it, but it was a lie.

My point is that **an attitude that says you can no longer trust someone at all if they've ever lied to you about anything is unrealistic.** I've met people who are so offended when they catch a family member in a very small lie that they consider it a major betrayal. I met a couple years ago who administered polygraph tests to their teenage children (the stepfather worked in law enforcement) to find out if they lied about coming home late.

If that's you, my suggestion is similar to what I said about fanatic parenting: **reconsider. You're not that righteous.** If you think you are, you're the problem—it's no wonder that your partner lies to you rather than face your indignation. They shouldn't, but if you examine how you treat them maybe you'll understand why they do.

Of course, I don't mean that lying to your partner is a good idea. I just mean that **there are degrees of bad**. Lying to your partner about bumming a cigarette and then admitting the truth in the same conversation is not the same as not telling your partner about being fired and inventing a cover story to maintain the lie for months. Both of those scenarios are based on couples I've met. In the latter case, the husband who pretended to still be employed was hoping to get another job quickly enough that he could just say he had changed jobs—which would be true, though obviously not the whole truth. His not telling his wife about being fired was partly about avoiding her anger, but also partly about sparing her worry. Both can be true simultaneously.

If you're the one who lied, I have a simple suggestion: **come clean, and don't do it again.** Whatever you did, it's worse when you lie about it. You'll just have to face your partner's reactions. Explaining to your partner that you deceived them to spare their feelings—even if it's partly true—doesn't go over well, as you can imagine if the roles were reversed.

Is this a deal-breaker? Not necessarily. **Couples can grow from situations like this and learn to trust themselves and each other.** So I put this in the growing pains category. As I noted in Chapter 5, that doesn't mean you should stay together. It just means you shouldn't break up in a panic about it.

Betrayal: Action Plan

If you're reeling from some kind of betrayal, whichever role you're in, your first priority is to calm down enough to be able to think about your options. This could mean seeking professional help from a therapist, clergyperson, or coach. It could mean getting legal or financial advice, not because you've necessarily decided to split up, but just to protect yourself if you're worried about what your partner might do. Or it could mean simply giving yourself some time to process what's happened, and letting yourself be uncertain for a while.

What's your next step? Write down your action plan.

Chapter 17

Addiction

Substance Issues

Scenario 14:
You're both in your late forties, and have been together for 25 years. You have a 22-year-old daughter together who left for college at 18 and has recently moved out permanently to another city.

When you first got together, you used to go out to bars with each other two or three times a week, both of you often getting at least buzzed and often drunk. You both cut way back on drinking when you were expecting your child, and your drinking habits continued to be light, averaging a drink or two once or twice a week, throughout her school years.

Since your daughter went away to college, one of you has been drinking more often, and it's become a concern to the other. You've had arguments about it. The arguments don't seem to resolve anything—you both end up feeling unheard and misunderstood. You're questioning whether you can stay together.

1. Are you in a similar situation, involving alcohol or any other psychoactive substance? Which role are you in?
2. If you're the one concerned about your partner's substance use, what are you worried about? Does your own family history or personal history of substance issues affect how you view your partner's use?
3. If you're the one your partner is concerned about, how do you understand their worry? To what extent do you share their concern?

Scenario 14: Suggestions

There are lots of resources available on the subject of addiction, many of which espouse contradictory understandings of what's going on. I'm not going to attempt to summarize the field. Let's focus on what you can do about your situation.

If you're the one whose substance use concerns your partner, you have (at least) two questions to consider.

First, **does your partner have a point?** Should you be concerned about your use? Most of the people I've worked with in situations like this recognize that they should at least cut back, if not stop altogether. They're recognizing that their use is problematic, though they usually disagree with their partner about how problematic it is. Ironically, the main effect of their partner's monitoring and complaining is to distract them from deciding for themselves if they need to change their usage patterns. Lots of people I've worked with have said that they know they need to stop using, not *because of* but *in spite of* their partner's wanting them to.

Second, whatever disagreements you might have with your partner's concerns, **how important is your continued use to you?** Is it worth the potential loss of your relationship? I'm not asking this rhetorically—I mean it as an actual question to consider. You could stop using for the sake of your partner's peace of mind, but if you resent doing so, your relationship won't improve. Or you could understand your partner's concerns as valid, even if your assessment is different, and stop using as an act of genuine generosity.

If you're the one who is concerned about your partner's use, you also have (at least) two questions to consider.

First, **does your partner have a point** when they insist that your concerns are overstated? I've met people who recognize that their own experiences with addiction, involving themselves or family members, have made them hyperalert to any sign of creeping addiction in their partner—perhaps leading them to panic about usage patterns that aren't necessarily problematic.

Second, if your partner disagrees with you about how problematic their substance use is, **can you learn to stop focusing on it, or is it a deal-breaker?** You've probably figured out already that **your attempts to monitor or control their use are not only ineffective, but counter-productive.** As I noted above, the attention you're giving the problem just distracts your partner from dealing with it. If you love your partner and want to continue living with them, you'll need to find a way to detach with love, as people in Al-Anon often point out. That means not arguing about your partner's use, and not intervening to protect them from consequences (though of course you'll intervene to protect others when necessary—detaching with love still means taking away the car keys if you have to).

Some couples I've worked with have tried an experiment. The partner who is concerned decides to give up on any attempts to influence the other partner's substance use—essentially, to try to detach with love—for some period of time. They recognize that the partner who is using can do whatever they want to do about their use, be it abstain, cut back, keep doing what they've been doing, or even use more—and they acknowledge that reality with their partner. Then they see what happens.

I've seen that experiment go various directions. Sometimes the using partner, freed from constant surveillance, makes dramatic changes in their use, and the concerned partner is genuinely relieved. Sometimes the concerned partner, freed from their constant vigilance, finds that they can just relax, regardless of what the using partner does. On the other hand, sometimes the experiment just confirms for the concerned partner that they are no longer willing to live with the using partner. You don't know unless you try.

The hardest part of that experiment is for the concerned partner to actually detach with love. It's not the same as just suppressing your objections. That's where groups such as Al-Anon (or Nar-Anon) can help.

If you can't detach with love—and many people can't—you'll either have to separate, or to resign yourself to misery as you wait for your partner to change. I don't recommend the latter option.

Gambling Issues

Scenario 15:
You're a hetero couple in your early thirties, married for six years, with your first child on the way. The man has become obsessed with one of the sports gambling apps. What started as a fun way of enhancing involvement while watching sports on weekends has turned into an intense daily preoccupation. You both have high-paying jobs, and the gambling losses haven't affected your ability to pay bills, but the woman is worried about where this might lead. When she found him streaming a ping-pong match at 3:00am so he could bet on each point, it turned into a screaming argument.

1. Are you in a similar situation? If so, which role are you in?
2. If you're the one concerned about your partner's gambling, what are you worried about? Does your own family history or personal history of gambling affect how you view your partner's use?

3. Are your joint finances at risk? Are there ways you've moved to protect them?
4. If you're the one your partner is concerned about, how do you understand their worry? To what extent do you share their concern?

Scenario 15: Suggestions
Gambling presents similar problems to substance use when it becomes addictive, and resources such as Gamblers Anonymous and Gam-Anon can be helpful.

The one additional caution I'd offer is that the non-gambling partner needs to protect their financial assets. One of the particularly insidious aspects of gambling addiction is that the gambler keeps thinking they'll make up their losses if they just keep playing—so they're apt to drain any resources they can access. If you want to heal the relationship, you'll need to separate your accounts.

Sex and Pornography Issues

Scenario 16:
You're a hetero couple, together for ten years. One of you, the woman, discovered that your partner has been masturbating to online porn several times a week. You consider this cheating, and your partner promised to stop, but you've now discovered that he has continued to do it when you're not home. You gave him an ultimatum: get treatment for this addiction or leave.

1. Are you in a similar situation? Which role are you in?
2. Whichever role you're in, do you consider masturbation cheating? Does it make a difference if porn is involved?
3. How might understanding this as an addiction help you find a solution? How might it interfere with finding a solution?
4. Would it make a difference if the online activity involved interaction with a real person (not just an image) on the other end?

Scenario 16: Suggestions

Whichever role you're in, there are two different issues I invite you to consider in this situation.

First, **do you consider the activity to be cheating, or objectionable for other reasons?** Is it a violation of your understanding of monogamy?

If you consider a partner's masturbation to be cheating, my suggestion is to rethink that stance, because it's not realistic. I've met people who are offended if their partner finds anything outside of their relationship to be a sexual turn-on. That's not only unrealistic, but it's actually harmful to a couple's intimate life, sexually or otherwise. **If you want to have a good sex life with your partner, you want your partner (and yourself) to be sexually alive.** There are all sorts of stimuli around, and some of them are hot. A healthy monogamous relationship means you can channel that heat toward each other, not that you have to be wrapped in insulation.

Even if you're clear that whatever your partner has been doing isn't cheating, you might still not approve of it. That's **where honest, open-minded conversation** can be helpful. Do you object to pornography in general as inherently demeaning to the people who make it? Is there room for multiple ideas about that? If you can **avoid ideological generalizations**, you might be able to come to some understanding of each other that will help put this issue in perspective.

Second, how helpful is the concept of addiction in dealing with this? I won't wade into debates about this, but simply note that I've seen situations in which it was helpful, and situations in which it wasn't helpful.

Labeling something as pathological is helpful to the extent that it guides you to treatment and support organized around the label. But labeling something as pathological can also have the effect of obscuring aspects of the situation that don't fit the label. Maybe your partner's behavior is an addiction, something that (by definition) they can't control, an illness rather than a moral failure. But maybe it reflects not illness, but disagreement—maybe they could control it, but don't want to.

Regardless of whether you consider your or your partner's behavior to be an addiction, you still need to decide if you want to stay together, and if so, how to do that without resentment in either direction. Couples therapy could be what you need.

Addiction: Action Plan

If you're the one concerned about your partner's behavior, can you detach with love, as Al-Anon describes it? Can you let go of your efforts to control what your partner is doing?

If you're the one your partner is concerned about, can you understand their concerns? How important is continuing to do what they're worried about? Could you give it up without resentment? Is it possible that it's an addiction, and that you need help to deal with it?

As I've defined the terms, addiction issues are growing pains, not inherent deal-breakers, since in theory it's possible to grow past them. But, as with any of the growing pains, that doesn't mean you have to choose to stay together. You've chosen to stay together this far, but you could decide to change that.

What's your next step? Write down your action plan.

Chapter 18

Relationships with In-Laws

In-Laws

Scenario 17:

You're a man and woman who have been married for eight years, and have two children, ages six and two. When your older child was three, the man got into an argument with the woman's father, which escalated to each saying the other isn't welcome in their home.

Since then, the woman has taken the kids to visit her parents, and sometimes asks her mother to babysit. The man had told his wife that he doesn't want the kids at his in-laws house if she's not with them—he doesn't think the kids are safe around their grandfather.

You've been arguing about this for almost three years, and lately the arguments have been getting more heated. You're each having doubts about the other's loyalty to your marriage.

1. Are you in a similar situation? Whatever the details, are you and your partner at odds about relationships with parents? Or might you be in the in-law role in a situation like this?
2. If you have children, how has the situation affected them?
3. If you're the partner who is cut off from an in-law, how well do you understand your partner's conflicted feelings? Have you been able to talk about that without getting defensive?
4. If you're the partner who is trying to maintain a relationship with a parent even though your partner won't, how do you manage your conflicted feelings? Have you been able to talk with your partner about it without getting angry?

Scenario 17: Suggestions

My main suggestion here is to **consider carefully the effects on your children and on your marriage** of prohibiting or limiting contact with their grandparent.

I'm guessing that whatever argument you, the man, had with your father-in-law wasn't about his safety around the kids. It was probably about the two of you being bull-headed.

Of course I could be wrong about that, but in the many instances of this I've seen, the safety concern the man is expressing only emerged after an argument. It's about his anger at his father-in-law, not about any actual substantive concern for the kids' welfare.

Do you think your wife is misguided in thinking that her father is safe around your kids? Unless you have good reason to believe otherwise, why would you doubt her opinion? She was raised by him. Yes, of course there are cases in which grandparents abuse grandchildren, sexually or otherwise. My point isn't that you should ignore that possibility. Rather, I'm saying that you need to **consider the effect of your anger on your judgment.** Just because he argued with you doesn't mean he's unsafe with your kids. You're not always a paragon of calm either. And letting your anger spill over into restrictions puts your wife in a horrendous position and threatens your marriage.

Scenario 18 (variation of 17):

You're the same couple as in Scenario 17, but this time the arguments are between the woman and her mother-in-law, and they stem from comments the mother-in-law makes about how you're raising your kids. Among other things, she has said she thinks you're too strict about dietary restrictions, too lenient about bedtimes, too tolerant of misbehavior in public, too controlling of their play—whatever you do that's different from what she did raising her kids, she's critical of.

If you're the woman in the couple, you've tried to get your husband to intervene, and he says he will, but he doesn't. If you're the man, you've tried to mediate between your wife and your mother, without success. You're each having doubts about the other's loyalty to your marriage.

1. Are you in a similar situation? Which role are you in? Might you be in the mother-in-law role in something like this?
2. How has this affected the children?
3. Whichever role you're in, how well do you understand each other's situation? Have you talked about it?

Scenario 18: Suggestions

If you, the woman, can **see your mother-in-law's comments as annoyances rather than crises,** you'll have some emotional room to maneuver.

In Chapter 11 I noted that how you parent your children is important, but not as important as we tend to worry it is. Your mother-in-law notices the ways you're doing it differently than she did, and perhaps interprets those differences as implicit criticisms of how she raised her kids. You hear her comments as explicit criticisms of how you're raising your kids.

My suggestion to both of you is recognize that your kids will be okay, or not, whether you do things your way or her way, as long as you're not truly horrible. And just being somewhat more permissive or somewhat stricter than you are isn't truly horrible. **Your kids are more resilient than most of us give them credit for.**

Your mother-in-law isn't the one reading this, but **if you can be curious instead of offended, you'll hear her comments as less threatening.** Maybe she even has a point sometimes—after all, she has more experience parenting than you do. But even if you don't agree with her, you might find it interesting to ask her about her own parenting style—where it came from, how she did it differently from how her mother did it, and whatever else you might wonder about.

Scenario 19 (variation of 18):
You're the same couple as in Scenarios 17 and 18, but this time the arguments are between the two of you. You, the man, have had a close relationship with your mother your entire life, especially since your mother divorced your father when you were eight years old. Since you moved with your wife to your present home, about a hundred miles from your mother, you've been talking with your mother two or three times a day.

You, the woman, initially had no problem with your husband's close relationship with his mother—in fact, it was one of the things that attracted you, since your relationship with your own mother was troubled. But soon after you got married, you and your husband were having an argument, and he called his mother and complained about you to her. She told him he should consider divorcing, and followed that up by texting you to say the same. She later backtracked on that opinion, but never apologized for expressing it.

In the years since then, the two of you have felt more and more disconnected. You, the woman, feel that your husband has no time for you, but always makes time for his mother. You, the man, feel caught between. You're each having doubts about the other's loyalty to your marriage.

1. Are you in a similar situation? Which role are you in? Might you be in the mother-in-law role in something like this?
2. How has this affected the children?
3. Whichever role you're in, how well do you understand each other's situation? Have you talked about it?

Scenario 19: Suggestions

My first suggestion is usually obvious with hindsight: **If you want your marriage to last, don't complain about your spouse to your parents or other family members.**

If you want to talk about being in pain from problems you're having in your relationship, talk about that—not about how awful your spouse is. Portraying your spouse as the villain of the piece might get you sympathy, but poisoning your family's view of your spouse won't help you in your marriage. If you need to talk to someone about the situation and aren't sure if you want to split up or not, talk to a therapist, not someone who has their own relationship with your spouse.

And if you're the in-law in this scenario, and your adult child is complaining to you about their spouse, you can offer sympathy, but your suggestions won't help. Again, this is usually obvious with hindsight.

When I've worked with couples in this kind of situation, I invite them to **focus less on the in-law and more on their relationship with each other.** When they've felt connected—in other words, when their intimate life has been fulfilling—then there's been plenty of room for close relationships with other family members and friends. When intimacy is lacking between them, then any intimacy offered to others just reinforces that lack. And the more that happens, the more they cause each other pain, and the barrier between them grows.

The problem the couple in our scenario faces isn't particularly about whether the man should involve his mother in disputes with his wife. They already know that's a bad idea. Their problem is that they've hurt each other so much that it seems futile to try to reconnect. When they consult me, they still want to try, but they don't know how.

If that's your situation—if you're feeling that reconnecting is futile, but you still want to try—then **your enemy isn't your partner,**

it's your sense of futility. (Cue FDR about the only thing to fear.) It's not certain that you can find each other again, but I've seen people do it. It's basically what I write about in *Betrayal and Forgiveness*. You'll need to find forgiveness, for yourself and each other, and then rebuild trust.

Relationships with In-Laws: Action Plan

My suggestions for the three scenarios in this chapter boil down to one question: Can you let go of needing to be right?

If you can, you'll need to figure out how to repair your relationships, not only with your in-laws but also with each other.

If you've cut off contact with an in-law, how might you start to re-connect? What would be a first step you could take in that direction? Can you discuss it with your spouse? Will this involve expressing some remorse for being part of the problem?

If you don't want to try re-establishing contact, how will you address this with your spouse? Have you talked about how the situation affects your spouse?

What's your next step? Write down your action plan.

Chapter 19

Religion and Politics

Religion

Scenario 20:
You're a couple in your mid-twenties, together for three years, no children yet, and you've decided to get married. You come from two very different religious backgrounds. You're both less involved in your religion than your parents and extended families are.

The parents of one of you are fine with your being together, but the parents of the other have made it clear that your marrying outside your faith tradition is painful. They haven't threatened to cut you off, but they've expressed the expectation that you'll raise your children in their tradition, and the hope that your partner will convert to their religion.

You haven't decided what kind of marriage ceremony to have, and you haven't decided what kind of religious traditions, if any, you'll teach your children.

1. Are you in a similar situation, or have you been in the past?
2. If you're the partner whose parents are less concerned, how do you understand your future in-law's concerns? Have you talked to your partner about the situation? How do you understand the pressures your partner might be experiencing?
3. If you're the partner whose parents are more concerned, what pressures do you feel? How well do you feel your partner understands those pressures? How do you understand your partner's experience? Have you talked to your partner about it?

Scenario 20: Suggestions

Of course, **you need to talk about these issues** with each other. How you'll handle the issues with your respective parents will follow from how you handle them with each other.

I'll offer a caution based on my conversations with hundreds of couples in similar situations, and based also on what I've heard from adults whose parents were from different religious backgrounds.

Some couples resolve the issue of what to teach the kids about their religious backgrounds by punting. They do little or nothing themselves at home, provide no religious education, and say they're letting the kids decide for themselves when they get older.

Don't do that.

There's no such thing as letting the kids decide for themselves. What you're doing if you leave it up to them is deciding that they'll be ignorant, and depriving them of experiences you can only have as a child: that is, the experience of being a child observing family traditions you inherited.

Whatever you do or don't do, you're imposing your decisions on your children. That's what being a parent means. That's not a bug, it's a feature.

I'm *not* saying you should insist on doing what either of your families did. If you object to how your parents raised you regarding religion, don't do what you object to. If your experience of your parents' religious observance was painful—and this is particularly associated with rigid, fundamentalist approaches—then it's not surprising that you'd want to spare your children that pain.

I *am* saying that a wholesale rejection of your family heritage can leave your kids floundering later on. I've talked with many adults who were left with the choice who felt that they were implicitly having to choose which parent they honored more. Or if their parents didn't seem to care about religion at all, they came to feel rootless, and often envious of people who were raised with a strong religious tradition.

There's no simple rule that solves these dilemmas. This is another example of needing to tolerate contradictory truths. **The key is to talk about it**, and agree on how to handle these issues consciously, rather than ignoring them.

Political Differences

Scenario 21:
You're both in your mid-forties, married for eighteen years, three school-age kids, both U.S. citizens by birth.

You've always leaned in different directions politically. But as the country polarized more and more in the past few years, you've found it difficult to talk to each other about anything political. Each of you consults news sources within your own political silo. What delights one of you enrages the other. You've been avoiding each other's social circles, because you've each gotten into screaming arguments with the other's friends.

Lately you're each having doubts about whether you can respect the other. How could anyone believe what they're believing? How could they be so ignorant, or dismissive, or cruel? You're worried about the future of your marriage.

1. Are you in a similar situation? If so, when did you notice it becoming problematic in your relationship?
2. Whether or not this is an issue in your primary relationship, are you in a similar situation with other family or close friends? Have you been avoiding some social contacts because of this?
3. Have you talked to your partner about the effects of your differences? I don't mean about the political issues—I mean about how your differences have been affecting your relationship.

Scenario 21: Suggestions

I'm old enough to remember the 1960 presidential election. My mother voted for Kennedy, and my father voted for Nixon. I remember them laughing about it on election day, as they realized they had each canceled out the other's vote. **There was no rancor, just amusement.**

As I recall, their friend circles included both Democrats and Republicans. Theirs was the generation that fought World War II. Whatever political differences they had were at the margins of general agreement that our political system was basically a good one.

I'm not suggesting that we go back to 1960 as a model of political harmony. Large chunks of the country had legal segregation, and efforts to change that were met with violence. There were deep divisions at many levels.

But it was rare that political differences came between couples. It's only recently that polls show that political differences are more of a turnoff than religious differences in terms of whom people would be willing to date.

What's changed?

My parents could view their differing votes in 1960 as representing different opinions as to who they think should be president. **They didn't view their votes as litmus tests of character.** They could still respect each other's basic decency even though they voted in opposite ways.

That's what's changed.

If you view someone's stance on a particular hot-button issue as a test of their character, you won't be able to talk with them meaningfully. Much of the political rhetoric we hear is aimed at casting people who disagree as at least wrong-headed and maybe evil. If your partner is on the other side, it's not simply that they've arrived at a different conclusion. It's that they're on the side of evil. That's why so many couples are coming apart over political differences.

If you can recognize that good people can differ on many issues—because those issues are complex and multifaceted—then you can be open to conversation across different opinions. Of course, to open yourself to other opinions can be scary. What if you change your mind? But if you can tolerate that anxiety, you have a chance to connect with others and come up with solutions that none of you would have come up with on your own.

In other words, **if you tolerate anxiety, you make intimate conversation possible.** Sound familiar?

Religion and Politics: Action Plan

Have you been able to talk to your partner about your differences with curiosity rather than contempt? Can you back away from your own ideological certainty and make room for that curiosity? Those are your challenges, whether you're dealing with religious or political differences.

What's your next step? Write down your action plan.

Chapter 20

Everything Else

What Else?

You've just looked at a range of potential problem areas in your relationship, and (I hope) come up with action plans to begin addressing the problems you identified.

If there are other areas we haven't touched on in Chapters 11 through 19, this is your invitation to work on them.

What else do you need to address with your partner? Create your own scenarios illustrating the problem, ask yourself relevant questions, come up with your own suggestions, and write an action plan as needed.

Take Action!

If you've been doing the work in this book, you now have a set of action plans.

Some of your action plans may simply note that there's nothing you need to do, because the topic is an area of strength, or at least isn't problematic. Others of your plans may be relatively easy to implement. And then there are the plans that fill you with dread.

My advice: **Start with the hard ones.**

Deal-Breakers vs. Growing Pains Revisited

In Chapter 5 I invited you to consider whether you should call it quits on your relationship or not. You've made it to this point in the book (presumably) because you're trying to fix it, not end it.

If your action plans call for working on your relationship, you've finished this book. Congratulations! Now it's about putting your action plans into practice. You've recognized that the problems you're dealing with are growing pains, which means you can solve them through growth. As I've pointed out before, you might still conclude that the growth you need to do involves splitting up—but you don't know yet.

And you might find that the growth you'll do with your partner leads you to a satisfying, meaningful, intimate relationship, better than you thought possible. I've seen it happen, and I hope it happens for you.

But what if you've concluded that your problems involve a deal-breaker?

If your action plans include splitting up—if you're convinced that efforts to stay together are doomed to failure, because no amount of growth can overcome the problems you're facing if you stay together—**then Chapter 21 is for you.**

Chapter 21

How to Split Up

Are You Sure?

This chapter offers some guidelines on how to split up. **As with all my suggestions, you may not agree, and there are often good reasons in particular circumstances not to agree. But at least consider them.**

But first, **are you sure you need to split up?**

As I noted in Chapter 5, if the problems you've identified are growing pains rather than deal-breakers, **don't break up too soon**. Make sure you've learned what you need to learn.

In particular, if you're dealing with infidelity, I urge you to reconsider before you decide to split up.

If you're the one having an affair and intend to leave your partner to make a life with that person, and you haven't told your partner about the affair, tell them before you decide to split up. You could discover that the resulting crisis forces growth that leads you to change your mind. And you're probably familiar with the phenomenon of rebound relationships, which rarely work out. Relationships that begin with deception, not surprisingly, are prone to trust issues.

If you've discovered that your partner is having an affair, and you still love your partner, take some time before you decide to split up. Give yourself a chance to get past the shock so you can think clearly about what you want.

That last guideline, to **give yourself a chance to get past the shock**, is generally a good one for any sort of betrayal. Of course, if you need to take immediate action to ensure your physical safety, or to protect your financial resources, you should do so, but even then you'll benefit from giving yourself time before you make a final decision on whether to split up permanently. **Decisions made in a panic are often regretted.**

You're Sure

If you're sure you want to split up, here are some dos and don'ts I've gleaned from working with couples.

Are You the Dumper or the Dumpee?

I'm assuming in this chapter that one of you is the dumper, and the other is the dumpee. I've met couples that made a mutual decision to split up, but it's rare. One of you is the one that pulled the plug.

By using that blunt terminology—dumper and dumpee—I'm inviting you to face that reality. Sometimes the person initiating the breakup tries to avoid their sense of guilt by insisting that the relationship was over anyway, and denies being the dumper. But if you're the one who made the decision, you're imposing something on your partner that they probably didn't want. You're the dumper.

The distinction between dumper and dumpee is not about who's right or wrong, or who's morally superior. If you're the dumper, you have reasons for doing it, and you have a right to do so. You've probably been in pain for a long time, and didn't decide to break up lightly. If you're the dumpee, you have reason to feel hurt by your partner's decision, and you probably need more time to accept what is happening.

But **neither of you is the villain or the victim.** If you think you are either of those, or think your partner is either of those, you'll have a hard time acting responsibly. There's plenty of blame to go around. But you're splitting up—arguing over blame won't help.

The Overall Guideline

Here's a guideline that applies in all situations:

Don't be a jerk, and don't be a doormat.

Both parts of that are important. You *both* have an interest in splitting up in a way that feels at least acceptable, even if not optimal, to *both* of you. That's obviously more important if you have children together, since you're going to continue to have a relationship going forward. But even if you don't have kids together, splitting up in a way that respects both parties' dignity is better for your soul than a win-lose ending, even if you're the winner.

The first part of the guideline, don't be a jerk, means that you should get hold of yourself before you act or respond in anger. **Take time before you fire off a response that will just make things harder.** Don't air your grievances on social media. Don't badmouth your partner to others. Yes, you're angry and in pain—you're still responsible for your own conduct. Apologize when called for.

The second part, don't be a doormat, means that you should be careful not to agree to something just to avoid disagreement. I've met people who were so eager to get a divorce over with that they agreed to terms they later came to regret. **Watch out for your own interests, even as you respect that your soon-to-be ex is watching out for theirs.**

Both parts of the overall guideline are important, regardless of whether you're the dumper or the dumpee. I've known people in either role who have been jerks and doormats—sometimes both. Don't be either.

Guidelines for the Dumper

Here are some guidelines that generally apply more to the dumper:

- **Don't try to justify or minimize your decision to your partner.** Don't try to convince your partner that it will be better for them to separate, even though that may turn out to be correct. Don't tell your partner that they deserve someone better for them than you—that's for them to decide.
- **Accept responsibility for making the decision, and don't get stuck in guilt.** Recognize that your partner didn't choose what you're doing, and hasn't had the time you've had to process the decision. Don't expect them to get over it quickly. Don't expect them to be cordial.
- **Don't give mixed messages.** For example, continuing to have sex with your partner might be fine for you, but cruel for them if it encourages them to believe you'll change your mind about leaving. Even if they say they've accepted that you're ending the relationship, they might be lying to themselves. Don't make it worse.
- Similarly, **don't try to be close friends with your partner, at least initially.** I don't mean be hostile, but until your

partner has had a chance to accept the new reality, your efforts to be a close friend won't help them. You're not the one who can help them feel better about losing you.

- **If your partner has been your financial adviser, or your chef, or your tech support, or your social activities coordinator, or your shoulder to cry on, stop using them for those things.** Again, it might be fine for you, but it's cruel for them.

Guidelines for the Dumpee

If you're the dumpee, here are some guidelines that apply more to you:

- **Don't try to talk your partner into changing their mind about splitting up.** The only effect it will have is to solidify their decision. Don't guilt-trip them, cajole them, browbeat them, or otherwise try to make them stay with you. I don't mean you should give up on *wanting* them to change their mind. But pressuring them won't work.
- **Focus on taking care of yourself, your children, your job, and whatever other responsibilities you have.** Cry when you need to, but carry on. You might not believe it yet, but you'll feel better sooner than you think.
- **Don't turn to your partner for comfort, even if they're willing to offer it.** Don't be hostile, but they can't be the one to help you accept losing them. Don't have sex with your partner, even if they offer—you're just making it harder to accept that they're leaving you.
- Find other people to talk to, but **don't badmouth your partner to anyone**, particularly if you have any hope of eventually reconciling. Try to accept that your partner has good reasons for feeling as they do, even if you wish they didn't.

- **Don't jump into another relationship yet.** Hang out with friends, but don't get romantically involved with someone until you can think about your ex, and maybe even talk with them, without feeling grief. (Yes, you'll violate this guideline, but don't say I didn't warn you.)

Guidelines for Both of You

These guidelines are especially for when you're working out agreements about things like custody and childcare arrangements, financial settlements, and other logistical issues.

- **Don't argue—just say what you agree or disagree with.** When you disagree, offer a counter-proposal. Don't be offended by a proposal you don't like; just don't agree to it. Don't ridicule your ex's proposals. Try to find some common ground.
- **Get legal and financial advice, and don't be offended that your soon-to-be ex also gets legal and financial advice.** Sometimes couples are worried that getting lawyers involved means a separation has to be hostile. It doesn't, especially if you're clear with your lawyer that you aren't out for blood.
- **Consider mediation**, which can help you get to an agreement you can both live with. Don't use mediation as couples therapy—focus on coming to agreement about logistical and legal issues.
- **Consider couples therapy**, which can help you learn to talk with each other to work through disagreements without freaking out. Don't use couples therapy as mediation—focus on emotional acceptance and mutual respect.
- **If you're coparenting, accept that the two of you will sometimes disagree about rules for your kids at your respective homes.** For example, your child might be

allowed a TV in their room at one house, but not at the other. Most of those differences don't matter to your child's wellbeing as much as you worry it does. Or even if you have strong feelings about something, the damage to your child from doing it the way your ex does it is almost certainly less than the damage to your child from having nasty arguments about it. **Get comfortable with not having as much say as you used to.** Your kids will be fine.

- **Be flexible about schedule deviations when you can.** Say no when you need to, and don't blame your ex if you say yes and then resent it.

- You already know this, but **don't use the kids as conduits for communication with your ex, and don't disparage your ex to the kids.** The kids should be able to enjoy time with either parent without feeling they're being disloyal to the other. That means you need to be okay with that yourself, which can be hard at first.

What's a Healthy Breakup?

If you're splitting up, can you visualize how you'd like to feel after some time when you've had a chance to heal?

One way to describe a couple who have healed from a breakup is that they have each come to forgive themselves and each other.

In saying they each have come to forgive, I don't mean restoring the relationship, or even restoring trust. I just mean that neither one is consumed by anger or pain or regret when they think of the other. They've accepted what happened as a valid part of their lives, appreciating the good times and grateful for the growth they experienced from the struggle.

I know exes who have gone on to establish cordial relationships with each other, even after a contentious divorce. I also know exes who still refuse to be in the same zip code decades later. Most of us would prefer to end up cordial. A lot of the work you've done in this book is to help you recognize that you can choose that outcome.

To heal after a breakup takes the same skill as to heal and stay together. Healing takes faith. Whichever direction you take in your relationship, may you move on with faith.

Acknowledgements

Most of what I've learned about helping couples heal has come from the couples themselves. I can't thank you by name, but if you've worked with me, you've been one of my teachers, and I'm grateful.

Thanks also to the many people who tried out the Stability and Intimacy Assessment and helped me refine it; to Sebastian Ryder, Seth Chalmer, and other readers of the prepublication manuscript; to my colleagues at Stone House Associates in South Burlington, Vermont, who have offered consultation and insight over many years; and to the guests we've had on our "Couples Therapy in Seven Words" podcast, over a hundred at this writing, whose ideas have broadened my perspectives.

My co-host on that podcast is my wife Judy Alexander. What I know about stability, intimacy, and joy in a marriage I know because of her.

About the Author

Dr. Bruce Chalmer is a psychologist and couples therapist with over 30 years of experience helping partners navigate the complexities of long-term relationships. Drawing on clinical insight, real-world compassion, and a deep understanding of how stability and intimacy intertwine, Dr. Chalmer has guided countless couples through the very challenges explored in *The Passion Paradox*. He is also the co-host with his wife Judy Alexander of the podcast "Couples Therapy in Seven Words," and is a trusted voice in relationship education.

Dr. Chalmer has served in leadership positions in several Vermont Jewish communities, and is also a musician, composer, and choral director. He and Judy have five adult children and six grandchildren.

For more information visit his website: brucechalmer.com.

Special Offer!

Dr. Chalmer offers workshops for couples and individuals. More information is at brucechalmer.com/workshops. **Enter the promotional code "Page193" when you sign up and get a 20% discount!**

www.ingramcontent.com/pod-product-compliance
Lightning Source LLC
Chambersburg PA
CBHW060459030426
42337CB00015B/1656